"An engrossing and enlightening version of this finest source of spiritual teaching in the world, [this book] expands the possibilities of conveying its wisdom even further into the Western world, as a greater number of people will now be able to readily grasp its message."

— *Spirit of Change*

"Working under the premise that there 'needed to be a truly different style of Gita,' organizational consultant Hawley created this prose version to speak afresh to Westerners. Hawley's rendition succeeds in its objective of providing 'clarity and flow' to the famous Indian poem. Hawley writes more as a disciple than a scholar, lending a devotional authenticity to the text."

— *Publishers Weekly*

"This well-researched composition stays true to the Vedantic philosophies that were first written down more than two millennia ago, while still providing an easily navigable text that will remain lively and interesting to Westerners well into the future."

— *Institute of Noetic Sciences Review*

"*The Bhagavad Gita* is unique among the great scriptures of the world as its appeal transcends the barriers of time and space. …Dr. Jack Hawley's walkthrough is not a mere translation; it is a sincere *sadhak's* presentation of the message of the *Gita* in a simple but insightful manner so that its perennial message goes home to Western readers. No one can 'walk through' this book without getting a deep insight into these everlasting principles given to all of humanity."

— V. K. Narasimhan, journalist and winner of India's Ramnath Goenka Award for Excellence in Journalism

"Reading this has been a soul-stirring, treasure-laden stroll. Eastern philosophy is captured in a lucid but profound manner for the pragmatic present generation of readers in the West, and in all countries."

— Venkatesh Varan, business consultant

"Dr. Jack Hawley has written this concise translation with his whole heart and mind obviously immersed in these timeless, practical, nonsectarian teachings. . . . He has beautifully preserved the meaning and intent of the verses in a simple, easy-to-read, and understandable language. Jack has a good grasp of even the most difficult passages. This is indeed a *Bhagavad Gita* worthy of belief and respect."

— Ram Prasad, executive director, American Gita Society

"I floated through it. . . . It filled in the whole picture for me, where I had just bits and pieces before."

— J. Narain, university vice-chancellor

"It's neither too cryptic nor too elaborate, but strikes a precise balance. There is not one sentence too many or too few. The broad, penetrating chapter on meditation is just perfect!"

— S. M. Nanjundaya, university administrator

"This rendition of the *Gita* will hold the reader's interest from the first to last page."

— Anil Kumar, university professor

"Stupendous. [Jack Hawley] has done a wonderful job."

— S. Raghavan, editor and international lecturer on
The Bhagavad Gita

"A great book which has truly affected my consciousness in the last few days as I read it. Thank you, Jack Hawley, for bringing this message more powerfully into my life. There is magic in it."

— Glenn Hovemann, publisher, Dawn Publications

THE BHAGAVAD GITA

A Walkthrough
for Westerners

JACK HAWLEY

NEW WORLD LIBRARY
NOVATO, CALIFORNIA

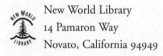

New World Library
14 Pamaron Way
Novato, California 94949

Copyright © 2001 by Jack Hawley, Ph.D.
Preface to paperback edition copyright © 2011 by Jack Hawley, Ph.D.

Text design by Tona Pearce Myers

Library of Congress Cataloging-in-Publication Data
Bhagavadgåitåa. English
The bhagavad gita : a walkthrough for Westerners / Jack Hawley.
     p. cm.
Includes bibliographical references and index.
ISBN 978-1-57731-147-7 (hardcover : alk. paper)
I. Hawley, Jack. II. Title.
BL1138.62.E5 B43 2001
294.5'92404521—dc21   00-013056

First paperback printing, March 2011
ISBN 978-1-60868-014-6
Printed in the USA on 100% postconsumer-waste recycled paper

g New World Library is a proud member of the Green Press Initiative.

20 19 18 17

Dedicated with a loving heart to
Sri Sathya Sai Baba

This is the Sanscrit symbol for *Om,* the primeval sound of the universe, the basic sound from which all else comes. *Om* is in every place, mind, and heart.

Often spelled *Aum*, it is usually spoken almost under the breath and pronounced in the consciousness as well as in the mouth as "Omm...." The small silence at the end is as important as the sound itself.

It is said that the recitation of *Om* while contemplating the mystical symbol will help to calm even the roaring waves.

CONTENTS

PUBLISHER'S PREFACE

When Mahatma Gandhi — the "great-souled one," the leader of India who nonviolently freed his country from British rule — died, a now famous photograph was taken of all his possessions: his simple white cotton piece of clothing, his glasses, his sandals, and his well-worn copy of *The Bhagavad Gita*. It was a book he read daily, a source of endless inspiration to him.

The *Gita* is read daily by millions of people in India, as well as throughout the world; it is in the homes of literally hundreds of millions of people, and is considered by a great many to be the finest source of spiritual teaching in the world.

When Jack Hawley presented us with this extraordinary prose version of it, which tells the story so clearly and beautifully, everyone in our company felt as if we had been given a great gift — one we feel blessed to be able to publish and share with the world.

There is endless wisdom and inspiration in these pages. The *Gita* has proven itself over hundreds of generations to be one of the greatest gifts ever given to humanity, one of the greatest scriptures ever written.

Read it straight through, as a magnificent story filled with great teaching. Or simply open it to any page at random, and ponder the words, applying them to your life experience.

This is more than a book, more than the writings of any mortal man or woman. It is Divine revelation, filled with the words of a vast, illuminated soul — and these words can lead you to a far greater life experience, and even to illumination itself.

Marc Allen
New World Library

PREFACE TO THE PAPERBACK EDITION

LESSONS LEARNED

*"The whole and sole purpose of the Bhagavad Gita,
the only reason it was
originally given to humanity,
is to help people rid themselves of their
worldly suffering, find true happiness and achieve
Self-realization."*
—— Sathya Sai Baba

Twenty-five years ago my wife and I were traveling across India's Deccan plateau in a non-air-conditioned taxi in the middle of summer. Late in the day, wet and wrinkled, we stopped at a modest guesthouse to quench our thirst and lay our heads on a pillow. Thirsting also for something to read, I noticed a lone book, *The Bhagavad Gita*, resting on the only shelf in the room. I had been introduced to this ancient text some ten years earlier and had read a few memorable excerpts, but the teachings had never gained a foothold in my awareness.

As I flipped through its dog-eared pages, I stopped at chapter seven where Krishna, the heroic Divinity figure of the *Gita's* story, begins to describe the very nature of the Divine. I was enthralled and began reading aloud to Louise, explaining that this was "God" talking:

I am Pure Consciousness, the underlying essence of all elements and beings.
I am the innate nature of everything.

In pure water I am the sweet taste.
In the sun and moon I am the radiance.
In the very center of human beings I live as virility and courage.

I am the slight, delicate scent, the sweet fragrance of the earth.
I am the brilliance in both fire and sun, and I am the light of Divinity in all beings.

I am the subtle spirit in spiritual practices that gives them their existence — the love in the devotee, the simple austerity in the ascetic, the sweet sense of charity in the giver.

This narrative on Divinity picks up several times throughout the book, but in those first few words of chapter seven we are plunged pleasantly into what has become a lifelong love affair with the wondrous *Bhagavad Gita*.

Since that encounter in the guesthouse, I have researched and written three books on the *Gita*. This one is the basis, the source, the reservoir of practical spiritual knowledge from which the others rise. Over these years we have traveled the world lecturing and doing workshops on the *Gita*'s teachings.

Five Beguiling Lessons

With the advent of New World Library's new paperback edition of the book, I would like to share some of things I have learned over the years.

1. I learned that there is a crucial difference between regular and spiritual reading.

This difference makes a *big* difference. Our everyday reading, which is part and parcel of living and working in the world, is primarily for gaining worldly information. Spiritual reading has loftier purposes — to reposition us beyond the worldly and lead us into spaces the mind could never imagine, to touch the Divine in each of us. We may skim during regular reading, but we need to approach our spiritual reading with a higher awareness.

I once met a young man in a local restaurant in India. His English was good but he had a thick European accent. I found myself leaning a bit closer to make sure I could hear. He told me how much he was enjoying reading and rereading my *Bhagavad Gita* book.

I asked how he liked the German translation. "Oh," he said, "I'm reading it in English — and I like reading it in English because it makes me think. If I was reading it in German, I would go through it too fast, like I always do, and then, when finished, I would fool myself that I had understood it. But that would not be true!

"Reading it in English, not my native language, makes me think about every idea and word, and ask myself, 'Do I truly understand this?' The extra work puts it deeper inside me, and I end up knowing it better."

We all zoom through our reading piles as he does. Whether the content is important or not, we click into a mindless, autopilot mode and thus take in a tiny percentage of what we skim. Speeding might be appropriate for most reading jobs, but speed kills spiritual reading. We have to lean a bit nearer to it.

2. **I learned that two of the points I made in the earlier edition need to be emphasized.**

First, contrary to its title, this book is not a simple "walk-through." When the book first came out, I wrote in the Introduction that the stroll may not be bump free. In retrospect, that wasn't clear enough. The book is written in easy English, but reading it entails positive effort. One reviewer said it's a book that asks much and gives back so much more. Moving through it is a great exercise for your spirit, and like any exercise, physical or soul based, you emerge in better shape.

Second, when I wrote the how-to-read-it pointers in the Introduction a decade ago, I conveyed the idea that getting the most out of this book is largely a matter of one's attitude and mood. At that time I *sensed* the importance of this, but now, having lived with the book in the real world, I *know* it! One's frame of mind while reading truly does make a difference. So when you read the Introduction (especially the last two paragraphs on page xxiv), inhale the suggestions — turn your reading into a receptive meditation.

3. **I learned that the spiritual journey is the central expedition of your life, and this book may well be the most important reading you ever do. Period.**

4. **I learned to communicate the *Gita*'s vastness by narrowing my own focal point.**

A few years ago I struggled mightily for days, weeks, trying to write an article on what the *Gita*'s splendor and utility mean to me. The prospect of composing yet another intellectual analysis or codification of the principles bored me. As I pondered, an ancient voice within me whispered, "Share your love." The *aha* doors opened....

I love the *Gita*'s basic goodness, and how it pushes me beyond merely striving to be a good person, toward becoming my own Divinity within. I love that it provides me with page after page of methods for calling forth that extreme goodness. And I love how it continually reminds me to do that.

I love my inner peacefulness whenever I enter the *Gita*'s teachings. I love how almost all my anger has been eliminated, and how worldly agitations are largely things of the past for me.

I love the *Gita* for its depth, its breadth, and mostly its height — the way it pulls me upward. I love it for its humanness as well as its sublimity.

I love the ultra-honesty in the *Gita* about religion — how it lives in the open space beyond religious dogma and yet embraces a reverence for the scriptural teachings of all faiths.

I love the *Gita*'s insistence that we consciously live by our own inner truth. I love how it doesn't compromise an iota on this, how it won't put up with any excuses where truth is concerned.

I love the *Gita*'s clarity about how we have to live with the consequences of our actions, good or bad, but with no hint of punishment. I love how it neither excuses nor overlooks humanity's dark side, and yet doesn't dwell there. Sanskrit, the precise, spiritual language of the *Gita*, has no word for *damnation*.

I love the antiquity of the *Gita*, appreciating that it precedes by thousands of years the societies we Westerners think of as the cradles of civilization. This isn't merely "older is better" snobbery. *The Bhagavad Gita* has passed the persistent tests of countless centuries, and yet it remains the basis for all the spiritual teachings known in the world today.

I love the *Gita*'s teachings on *acceptance* — not mere compliance, but acceptance as an overpowering state of mind and way of being, a receptiveness so elevated that one's life forever soars when touched by the magic of it. This all-embracing acceptance is the most shining facet of love, the very essence of spiritual surrender.

I love the happiness in the *Gita* and thoroughly appreciate its careful explanation of how to attain real bliss. I also appreciate that it lays out what happiness is not and is so clear about the pitfalls in the way of lasting happiness.

I love that the all-powerful Divinity described in the *Gita* is loving and nonpunitive.

I love that the *Gita* looks death (and life) squarely in the eye and offers a straightforward system for not just conquering our fear of death but triumphing over death itself!

Finally, I love the *Gita*'s emphasis on *application* rather than airy theology — insisting that putting the teachings into practice will lead to a happier, more graceful life.

5.   I learned that there's an enthralling paradox in all this.

In the final analysis, it's not about this book, and it's not even about the brilliant, never-changing principles and teachings of *The Bhagavad Gita* itself. It's about *you*. It's about you, learning to rid yourself of your worldly suffering and find true happiness. It's about you, learning to slip quietly into your own True Self Within. The only real destination in life is your inner Divinity. In the end it's all you have.

INTRODUCTION

WHY THE BHAGAVAD GITA?

"Ancient, but strangely close and familiar...."

The *Gita* is an epic mystical poem about life, death, love, and duty from the peoples who settled in the river valleys in southern Asia and developed a sophisticated culture thousands — probably scores of thousands — of years ago. It is a half-inch-thick poem embedded in the middle of a six-inch-thick poem, the *Mahabharatha,* a literary masterpiece about the heights and depths of the human soul.

The Bhagavad Gita contains the inner essence of India, the moral and spiritual principles found in the very earliest scriptures of this ancient land. One of them, the *Rig Veda,* is said to be the oldest record of humankind! To read *The Bhagavad Gita,* therefore, is to reach countless epochs back in time — and yet, as I settled into these cobwebby teachings, they felt strangely close and familiar. It was as if some force could at long last take my hand and walk me down a not-so-quiet path to important and meaningful truths; as if I — this too-worldly Western businessman living behind the fading whitewashed walls of an ashram in southern India — could now, finally, be let in on the most profound secrets of humankind.

This ancient tome is not, as one might expect, about withdrawing from life to meditate in some far-off cave. It's more of a manual to clutch close, a friendly guide for living a more spiritual life today — a more purposeful and fulfilling life even while staying fully active in the world. The *Gita* is very much about how to remove sorrow and pain from life and thus achieve contentment and serenity, which is a wondrous goal. But even more than that, it's about the absolute highest prize: liberation and self-realization in this lifetime. It's not merely about the quest for these lofty things; it's a detailed map to the treasure itself — a handbook for living a higher, more satisfying existence here, now, in today's tough and troubling times.

And the *Gita* is also about how to die, and what happens after.

As I studied the *Gita,* I found myself so engrossed in this old yet current scripture that I carefully worked through each of the 700 verses (*slokas*), one by one. I called it a "walkthrough," and it was not an easy stroll. The *Gita's* message is full of profound, sometimes intricate spiritual concepts. Many of the painstaking translations, written by scholars for other scholars, can be almost painfully thorough. And Sanskrit, the early language of the *Gita,* contains exact terms for spiritual and philosophical concepts that, when put into English, can sound too condensed — like one of those old pay-by-the-word telegrams ("Arrive Noon Tuesday Meet Me"). Important details are missing; you often don't know what is really being said.

I wanted to understand the book in a way that spoke as directly as possible to my struggles and daily concerns, so I developed a pattern of juggling five or six translations of the *Gita* on my desk and lap, scratching notations in the margins, checking one against the other, and writing out my own synthesis of each *sloka* in modern American English. This allowed me to get into the flow of ideas and not interrupt my reading every few words to clarify the meaning of some hard-to-grasp idea. I ended up working my way through thirty-some versions, many over 1,000 pages, several consisting of two or three volumes (one was seventeen volumes).

It wasn't as onerous or bookish as it sounds because over the years I had already developed a relationship with the *Gita*. Although my cultural background (as a practical organization consultant from California via upstate New York) is far distant from India, for me the *Gita*'s teachings were tangible and immediate. For twelve years my wife, Louise, and I had lived about six months each year in a spiritual community in rural India where the culture of the *Gita* is still a strong part of daily life. I was therefore able to test these teachings on the touchstone of life's trials as I lived them.

As each day closed, I would read my notes to Louise, who had also grown to love this great work, to see if the day's writings made sense to another ordinary, interested Westerner. We looked forward to these nightly sessions, and as we grew to better understand the *Gita*, we developed an even greater admiration and trust of it.

Dusting off the *Gita*'s gems of wisdom and adding them to the necklace of our daily living changed us and beautified our lives (and perhaps our immersion in the *Gita* even saved Louise's life, as I explain in the Afterword). There is a humility that comes with rediscovering these old pearls that have touched countless millions of souls through many thousands of years. And there is an awe at seeing how germane they are to the problems of today's world.

The "walkthrough" metaphor contained more than I had envisioned. At first it just felt like a friendly term implying an ease of reading. But as the work progressed, my task became more evident: this needed to be a truly different style of *Gita*. The traditional way of imparting these ancient truths is to present a short, aphorism-like teaching (a "telegram phrase"), and then explain it through several pages of in-depth "commentary."

That process is too lumbering for today. This needed to be a livelier *Gita,* more attuned, a *Gita* that could be read from cover to cover without backtracking to recall certain words, or sidetracking into companion volumes to find out what it really means. This *Gita* had to stand on its own two feet, without crutches of any kind. The whole point is to take your time, walk through it from beginning to end, and enjoy the stroll.

Thus I found myself even more intensely juggling the many resource books, making sure that in the end I could stroll easily, and Louise could listen smoothly, with understanding. I had to repeat the meanings of unfamiliar words, and restate several times the explanations of certain ideas that are used quite differently in the *Gita* than we Westerners use them (the definition of *reality*, for example). I chose to repeat these clarifications as asides or in parentheses so the reading would continue to flow.

"Clarity and flow" became my mantra as the work developed, but I also had to ensure that it did not turn into just another interesting self-help book — that it retained its very special energy and remained a full-strength, undiluted *Gita.* I tested the manuscript with several people who are knowledgeable of Sanskrit and the *Gita,* including professor friends who are not at all shy about giving criticism. Some wrinkled their brows ("just for Westerners?"), but after getting into it they all liked it and offered many suggestions. A few even confessed that they had personally learned much from it. Not one of them found the frequent reminders too repetitious. Indeed, Krishna, the God figure in the *Gita,* restates the same truths again and again in different contexts and imageries — like a mother repeating lessons to her child.

That's how it unfolded. In this quite natural way, this new version of *The Bhagavad Gita* shuffled happily into being — a concise but powerful book that invites ancient but strangely close and familiar ideas into our lives, and gives us new understanding of ancient truths.

Timeless, Pure Truth

To read *The Bhagavad Gita* is to swing back and forth smoothly between the head and heart, between the worldly and the spiritual, arching between gaining knowledge and applying it in today's real world. In this swing from humanness to godliness lies the *Gita's* secret penetrating power, its ability to lift and move us.

The year is 3141 B.C.E. Arjuna, an esteemed warrior-prince at the height of his powers, the greatest man of action of his time, is readying to go into battle. It is a righteous fight to regain a kingdom rightfully his. All his life he has been a courageous, successful achiever, renowned for prowess in combat. But now, on the eve of the biggest clash of his career, an odd thing happens. His hands begin to shake.

Arjuna is in his magnificent war chariot pulled by four white steeds. The chariot driver, Arjuna's best friend from boyhood, is Krishna, an *Avatar,* an incarnation of Divinity on earth. Arjuna, who doesn't really understand Krishna's Divinity, has directed him to drive the chariot into the center of the plain where the great battle is soon to begin. The opposing armies have gathered on each side.

It is an epic scene: two lone figures parked between the legions of good and evil; masses of soldiers, tents, cook fires, neighing horses, banners snapping in the early-afternoon breeze; the bustle, noises, and smells of pre-battle filling the air.

Arjuna's eyes scan the opposing forces, pausing on former friends, revered uncles, teachers who taught him his warrior skills. All are bravely making ready for the mutual slaughter. He slumps, breathes heavily, and looks quizzically at Krishna.

Reading the *Gita*, we come to better understand life as an inner battle, a struggle for the mind, heart, body, and spirit. And, make no mistake, it is a fight to the death. We learn that our real enemies are not outside but within: our own desire, anger, and greed. This is what makes it so hard. These arch-enemies have linked forces so powerfully that they are all but unbeatable. We're losing.

The *Gita* boldly declares that spirituality is the only winning solution. Turn inward, it directs us, and upward. Look no further than the True Self Within.

> Seated in his chariot in the middle of the battlefield, the slumping Prince Arjuna, his voice barely audible, asks, "Why am I doing this, Krishna? Life is so cruel, so demanding. I don't know if I have the heart for battle anymore." His eyes fill with tears, his knees soften, and he sinks deeper into the vehicle seat. "Beloved friend," he says, "please tell me — what is it all about?"

Like water that filters slowly down through earth and comes out fresh and pure, important ideas passing down through the sands of time are eventually rubbed clean and emerge as pure truth. Although stated in different ways at different times by different peoples of the world, these truths have been known to humanity for centuries, for millennia. Though all races and eras may have their own conceptions of God, they all do have God, and Truth, and Goodness. All higher religions and philosophical systems are in nearly complete agreement with these basics.

The Bhagavad Gita is one of the earliest, clearest, and most comprehensive statements of these perennial truths. In the *Gita*, the Divine comes to His friend man in the middle of a vicious war and carefully expounds the laws and principles that govern human life.

> We see Arjuna on the battlefield, this impressive warrior, bent, burdened, eyes glistening, pleading for the meaning of life. Krishna, totally calm, responds in effect, "Oh,

you really want to know?" With that, he takes the next twenty minutes to deliver the answer — straight from the Source!

The *Gita's* eighteen chapters can be divided into three clusters. The first six chapters focus mainly on knowing the True Self and, concurrently, on the need to perform one's worldly duties effectively for society's welfare. The next six concentrate on the very nature of the Godhead, and the great love for Him that springs from intimately knowing Him. The final six provide particular knowledge and wisdom for achieving the very purpose of existence, which is to liberate ourselves from the inevitable pain and sorrow that life deals us and ultimately to merge into that Godhead, Divinity itself.

All these are ideas of extraordinary size and power, with numerous subtleties and shades of thought. Krishna presents each of these huge ideas gradually, piece by piece, chapter after chapter, until the whole picture becomes clear.

Imagine! A man we can all identify with is in dire straits, at a crossroads, brought to his knees by the great pressures and complexities of life, shakily reaching out. And his best friend, an incarnation of God, takes his hand and walks him through the answer — explaining step-by-step the most profound secrets of all ages.

Walking through the *Gita* may not be bump free. Some words are unpronounceable and some of the ideas are so new to us or so different to our Western culture they can be missed, or worse, dismissed. The idea of *Atma,* for example, which is the Divinity in us, can feel strange to a Westerner ("me, God?") until *Atma* is understood to be a version of the soul. The ideas of *detaching* and *surrendering* are anathema to most Westerners. For some, the concept of *Avatar* (an embodied God) is unthinkable; for others it is acceptable only if it happens to be *their* idea of God who inhabits a body.

Early in the story most readers agree with Arjuna's antiwar sentiments, only to be dismayed when Krishna, seeming to justify war, tells him to go and fight! The shock diminishes as we gradually learn that it is not a question of being for or against war, or even an issue of slaying or being slain, but an issue of living by one's inner truth and doing one's duty. We have to keep reminding ourselves that the battle is metaphoric, that the war is being fought inside each of us and will continue throughout our lives.

There are bound to be other bumps. Many of the words in the original Sanskrit have multiple meanings (*karma*, for example), and some of the concepts may not appear fashionable in our times (*sacrifice, duty,* and *purity* are examples). There will probably be others.

The point is to try not to be turned off or dismiss anything in the *Gita* too early. These truths have survived the sands of time; what remains is amazingly pure and practical. This is a powerful work filled with Truth beyond intellectualization.

You have to read the *Gita* through your heart. It is your mood while reading that smoothes your way through this ancient scripture. Be as receptive as you possibly can. Toss uneasiness and skepticism on the shelf for a while. Try to suspend hasty judgments, and be more patient with unfamiliar usage of familiar words. Allow new conceptions of unity and Divinity to enter and expand you into new ways of thinking, and of being. Read it heedfully and be prepared to take contemplation breaks along the way. Let it sink in. There is a high magic in reading this way.

The magic resides in the reader's overall attitude. This mood of acceptance is precisely how the *Gita* exhorts us to live our lives. This is the invaluable state of mind that brings a happier life! When we imbibe these ancient teachings in this spirit, its high message seeps into our being, prompting and penetrating every thought and act. It becomes a part of us, and we of it. Thus the process of reading the *Gita* becomes an actual experience of the profound truths it brings. Reading it this way is *being* it!

The *Gita*, after all, is not theology or religion — it's poetry. It's a universal love song sung by God to His friend man. It can't be confined by any creed. It's a statement of the truths at the core of what we all already believe, only it makes those truths clearer, so they become immediately useful in our daily lives. Those truths are for our hearts, not just our heads.

The *Gita* is more than just a book, more than mere words or concepts. There is an accumulated potency in it. To read the *Gita* is to be inspired in the true sense of the term: to be "in-spirited," to inhale the ancient and ever-new breath of spiritual energy.

Now, we too are there on that long-ago yet strangely current battlefield, a witness to Krishna's grand teachings. We too are there, being let in on the secrets. We watch and listen as the Lord Himself, swinging easily between ecstasy and practicality, imparts the absolute deepest and highest teachings. We too are walking through God's precise, loving responses to the most anguishing and important questions of humanity today.

Part 1

KNOWING THE
TRUE SELF WITHIN,
AND SELFLESS ACTION

CHAPTER 1

ARJUNA'S ANGUISH
(*Arjuna Vishada Yoga*)

*"Why should I wage a bloody war?...
Death would be better for me!"*

His unseeing eyes blinked several times as he spoke to his minister Sanjaya. The blind old king, Dhritarashtra, fidgeted and cleared his throat. "Tell me, Sanjaya, what is happening on the holy plain where the mighty armies of my son, Duryodhana, and the armies of his cousin Arjuna are gathered to fight?"

The old man knew that his son Duryodhana's decision to go to war was wrong. He knew that the young king's judgment was clouded over by his jealous hate for his cousin. The old man had felt pangs of conscience but had said nothing when his son cheated Arjuna's family out of their rightful kingdom and then denied their requests for even a trifling parcel of the land that was rightfully theirs. The old man had maintained his curious silence when his son mortified Arjuna's wife and the whole family in public by having a henchman attempt to strip her of her clothes. He didn't condemn his son's heinous attempt to assassinate Arjuna's entire family. Nor did the old man try to change his son's mind when the young king sneered at all the recent peace overtures from Arjuna's family.

Indeed, the old man was so caught up in his mindless support of his son that neither ethical nor spiritual feelings could find their way into his heart. All good judgment had been lost. An unfair and ill-conceived war was about to erupt, and though he was the only person who could at this point avert the disastrous slaughter, he had no mind to do so.

2 The minister Sanjaya, because of his honest character, had been granted temporary *yogic* powers to see and hear what was occurring on the distant battlefield. (Sanjaya's name means "victorious over the self.") With a steady voice he replied to the old king's question: "Your son, King Duryodhana, is now viewing for the first time Prince Arjuna's opposing army all drawn up and ready to fight. It is obviously more formidable than Duryodhana had expected and he seems a bit anxious. Your son turns to his own forces as if looking for something or someone. Almost childlike in his manner, he finds Drona, his old archery teacher, in the crowd and moves quickly to him."

Sanjaya paused and leaned toward the old man, "Why is your son running to his former teacher? Perhaps his confidence wanes, or his conscience bothers him."

The old king didn't immediately react to this, which   3
to Sanjaya showed that the old man's spirits were as
sinister as his son's. Sanjaya continued his description
of the distant scene: "Your son, almost flinging his
words at his venerable teacher, says, 'Well, Drona,
take a look at the army marshaled by your talented
disciple, Arjuna. Why did you accept him as your
pupil and teach him the arts of war?' The question
carries a taunt, implying that Drona had made a mistake years ago in tutoring this prince who is now the
enemy."

Sanjaya shook his head, "No one should ever speak to
his teacher this way; it reveals your son's nervousness."

Without waiting for the old king's reactions, Sanjaya   4–6
continued his account: "Your son is now mentioning
the names, one by one, of the noted leaders of Arjuna's
opposing army, some of whom were also Drona's students. He is too carefully enunciating each name,
which is an indirect but rather obvious censuring of
his ex-master for the opposition's great strength.

"But now your son realizes that he has overstepped his   7–8
bounds and switches to listing the leaders on his own
side. He puts the teacher Drona at the top of his list,
clearly a patronizing gesture. As your son continues
speaking, the generals standing close by appear
uncomfortable with the too careful way he is voicing
their names."

Sanjaya waited a moment, as though continuing to   9–10
watch the far-off scene, and then resumed his
account. "Sensing his generals' discomfort, your son
abruptly stops. 'But we have many heroes on our
side,' he says, 'and they're ready to lay down their lives

for me!' But again his words don't fit his demeanor. There's a forced bravado in his voice; it's not clear whether he's putting down his own army or the opposition's. It's as though your son is unwittingly spelling ruin to himself and our forces even as he attempts to put weakness on the enemy.

11 "He tries to rectify this, and blurts an order to his generals, 'Go, assume your positions,' he says and then adds, 'But at all costs protect Field Marshal Bhishma.' His words and manner again reveal doubts, as if he does not trust his own generals. Or perhaps his concern about protecting Bhishma, the venerable old man both sides call 'grandfather,' is a grasp at a semblance of righteousness for his own side."

12 Sanjaya stopped talking as he watched the events unfold on the distant battlefield, and then resumed his narration: "Now, Bhishma, as if trying to cheer your son and rescue the deteriorating situation, is suddenly roaring like a lion and blowing his conch, indicating that the battle has begun!

13 "All the armies standing behind him have suddenly come to life, blaring forth their conches, kettle drums, cymbals, cow-horns, and trumpets. It's a loud, tumultuous noise.

14–15 "Now the opposition, led by Prince Arjuna and his lifelong friend Krishna, are answering this deafening roar with long, wailing blasts on their own conches.

16–18 "This incites all their forces to join in trumpeting and pounding drums — a noise that fills earth and sky with reverberations. The tumult seems even greater than that of the army of your son, although Arjuna's army is smaller.

"Like thunder, the noise of the opposition seems to 19
tear through the hearts of your son's armies. It's as if
the respective clamors of the two sides echoes the relative justness of their causes. The opposition's greater
commotion seems to abnormally penetrate the hearts
and consciences of your forces."

Arjuna Loses His Resolve

The old blind king squirmed in his seat, but ever- 20–23
honest Sanjaya ignored it, and continued his commentary. "Your son's blood enemy Prince Arjuna,
aware that the fighting is about to begin, lifts his bow
and speaks with an obvious — perhaps too obvious —
zeal. 'Krishna,' Arjuna says, 'place my chariot between
the two armies! I want to view those who come here
daring to fight for the evil-minded Duryodhana.'

"Everyone on both sides watches as Krishna drives 24–25
Arjuna's splendid war chariot onto the open field
between the two armies and positions it in front of the
opposing generals. 'Behold the gathered foes,' Krishna
says with an edge in his voice.

"Arjuna now looks long at both armies, staring espe- 26–28
cially at his paternal uncles, teachers, cousins, and various benefactors, friends, and comrades on both sides.
As his eyes fall on those who are now his enemies, his
attitude seems to waver and he appears confused. He
begins to speak to Krishna but the words get caught
in his throat. The prince collects himself and again
begins, 'Seeing my kinsmen gathered here ready to
fight,' he says, 'all of a sudden I am overwhelmed by
my emotions.

" 'My arms and legs feel heavy, Krishna. My mouth 29–30
is dry and my hair stands on end — and my body is

shaking. See!' Arjuna holds out his hand and even he is surprised at the forcefulness of his tremors. He clears his throat and continues, 'I can hardly hold my bow. My skin burns all over. My mind whirls. I can barely stand up. What is happening to me?'"

31-32   With this indication of Arjuna's weakness, a slight smile formed on the old king's face. Sanjaya noticed it and continued his account. "Arjuna takes a deep breath and speaks, 'I see bad omens for our side, Krishna. I can't see any good coming from slaying my relatives. This is unlike our earlier days of glory, Krishna, old friend. Now I don't desire victory, or a kingdom, or pleasures. Of what use are they? Of what use is life, Krishna?

33-35   "'It is for the sake of the people on our side — our own teachers, relatives, and allies — that we seek the pleasures of victory and kingdom. Here they are in battle gear ready to give up their property and even their lives. It's all so useless, Krishna. Even though these enemies want to kill me, I don't want to kill them — not even for the kingship of the whole world or even the heavens. If these great prizes hold no interest for me, why should I wage a bloody war for this paltry kingdom?

36-37   "'I would be forever ashamed, Krishna, if I were to kill my kith and kin. I could never find any satisfaction in such slaughter. Though their bows are drawn to kill, to slay these people would be a sin. So what if they're evil? They're my relatives. How could I ever again be happy?

38-39   "'I know they are overcome with greed. And I know they are blind to the evil in all their treachery. But does that justify my being blind too?

" 'Old friend,' Arjuna continues to Krishna, 'when a 40–41.
family declines, its traditions are destroyed, and the
entire family loses its sense of oneness. Without unity,
the women get corrupted, and with the decline of
women the world is plunged into chaos.

" 'Social turmoil is hell, Krishna, for the family, for the 42–45
destroyers of the family, and for the whole society. It
is said that those who destroy family unity have to live
in hell. Ah! And yet here am I, goaded by greed, ready
to kill my own kinsmen!

" 'Krishna, if those same relations attack me and kill 46
me, unresisting and unarmed on this battlefield, so be
it. Death would be better for me!' "

At those final, labored words of Arjuna, Sanjaya 47
stopped his commentary for a moment and then told
the blind old king what he saw. "Now, the great warrior Prince Arjuna, overcome by anguish in the middle
of the battlefield, slumps to his chariot seat and flings
his bow and arrows to the floor of the chariot."

CHAPTER 2

THE PATH OF KNOWLEDGE
(*Sankhya Yoga*)

"... the cessation of your pain and sorrow will depend on how well you overcome your ignorance of your True Self that lives within you."

Arjuna's eyes were burning with tears of compassion and confusion. The blind old king was rejoicing, thinking an easy victory was at hand. Sanjaya continued his straightforward report of the distant battlefield: 1

As Krishna watches the once-brave warrior prince plunge into pitiable weakness His normally soft eyes become steely, and He speaks. "Arjuna, where does all this despair come from? This egoistic self-indulgence at a time of crisis is shameful and unworthy of you. You are a highly evolved, cultured man who is supposed to live a truth-based life, a life of *dharma*. And yet your 2 confused mind is unbalanced and would not know truth if it hit you over the head.

3   "I know you are astounded at My lack of commiseration, but you must not yield to this feebleness! Truth and right can never be obtained by the weak. You are a great warrior, a proven winner. Cast off this faint-heartedness. Stand up, O scorcher of enemies!"

4-5   Arjuna interrupts: "I can't believe you're telling me to fight!" He shakes his head as though trying to clear his mind. Krishna sits quietly. Arjuna breathes deeply and blurts, "How?" The word hangs in the air between them. "How?" he repeats, "How can I *not* be weak, Krishna? For me to attack Bhishma, who has been like a grandfather to me, and assault my beloved former teacher Drona, would be wrong! I should revere these elders, not shoot at them. I don't want a blood-smeared victory.

6   "If I kill them, I would not care to live, Krishna. It would be better to be killed myself. Ah," he mutters ruefully, "I don't know which way to turn. Either way, winning or losing this battle, I lose."

Arjuna Becomes the Disciple, Krishna the Divine Teacher

7-8   "I'm utterly confused," Arjuna continues, "as to what is my duty. I can't think of any remedy for this awful grief that has dried up my energy, Krishna. If I were to gain great wealth and power, what would that prove? I'm asking you to help me, not to just tell me to go out and fight. I beg you to tell me what I should do. I am your pupil; be my teacher, my *guru*. I take refuge in you and surrender to you. Please instruct me, beloved Krishna, show me the way."

The great warrior-prince, who has never known 9
retreat, slips deeper into his dark dejection. He mumbles, "I shall not fight," and becomes silent.

Now that Arjuna has submitted himself as a pupil, 10
Krishna transforms into His true role as the Divine
Teacher. He tightens the reins in His hand, looks long
into the crestfallen warrior's eyes, and begins to speak.

"You may grieve sincerely, Arjuna, but it is without 11
cause. Your words may seem wise, but the truly wise
one grieves neither for the living nor the dead!

"There has never been a time when I, or you, or any 12
of these kings and soldiers here did not exist — and
there will never be a time when we cease to exist.
Physical bodies appear and disappear, but not the
Atma (the soul, the life force) that lives within them.

"This life force comes and dwells in a body for a 13
while. While therein, it experiences infancy, childhood, youth, and old age, and then, upon death, passes
eventually to a new body. Changes such as death pertain to the body, not the *Atma*. The wise person does
not get caught up in the delusion that he or she is this
body, Arjuna. This delusion is the very definition
of *ego*.

"Arjuna, the contact of bodily senses with objects and 14
attractions in the world creates feelings like sorrow or
happiness, and sensations like heat or cold. But these
are impermanent, transitory, coming and going like
passing clouds. Just endure them patiently and bravely;
learn to be unaffected by them.

"The serene person, unaffected by these worldly feel- 15
ings and sensations, is the same in pain and pleasure,

and does not allow him- or herself to get disturbed or sidetracked. *This* is the person fit for immortality. Realize this and assert your strength, Arjuna. Do not identify your True Self merely with your mortal body.

16   "*Real*, as used in spirituality, means that which is eternal, never changing, indestructible. This is the very definition of 'Reality.' That which is Real never ceases to be. Anything that is impermanent, even if it lasts a very long time and seems durable, eventually changes and thus does not have true Reality. The wise ones understand the difference between the Real and the not-Real. When you fully understand this profound fact, you will have attained the zenith of all knowledge.

"One's body, according to this logic, is not Real. And yet, there is something that dwells within the body that is Real: the *Atma* — which is existence itself; awareness, pure consciousness.

17   "Get to know this Reality. It pervades the entire cosmos and is unchanging and indestructible. No power can affect it. No one can change the changeless.

"This *Atma*, Arjuna, is like space or sky. Clouds appear in the sky but their presence does not cause the sky to grow apart to make room for them. In the same manner, the *Atma* (the True Self Within) remains ever itself. Things of the material universe come and go, appear and disappear, but the *Atma* never changes.

18   "Only the body is mortal. Only the body will come to an end. But the *Atma*, which is the True Self Within, is immortal, and will never come to an end. So fight, O Warrior!

"You talk about killing or being killed; know that the   19
body may be killed but the indwelling Reality (the
Atma) can never be. To say that one person slays and
the other is slain may be correct from a physical
worldly standpoint, but it is not the Reality of the
matter.

"The *Atma*, this Real us, was never born, nor will it   20
ever die. In fact, this eternal Reality within is never
destroyed; it never undergoes any changes. When
your ego takes over and you erroneously identify yourself with the body, you feel that physical death is death
to the self, and that is frightening. But the Self (*Atma*)
can never be 'killed.' When the body is slain the *Atma*
remains unaffected.

"The one who understands this hard-to-grasp prin-   21
ciple of *Atma* — the True Self Within that is eternal,
indestructible, and changeless — realizes that at this
level of comprehension there is no 'slaying' and no
'causing another to slay.'

"As a person sheds a worn-out garment, the dweller   22
within the body casts aside its time-worn human
frame and dons a new one.

"The Indweller — the Self, *Atma* — remains unaf-   23–24
fected by all worldly changes. It is not wounded by
weapons, burned by fire, dried out by wind, or wet by
water. This indwelling Self is all-pervading (which
means it is everywhere). It is also eternal and changeless because it is beyond the worldly dimension of
time — time has no access to it.

"Arjuna, the cessation of your present pain and sorrow
will depend on how well you overcome your ignorance of your True Self that lives within you."

The Qualities of the Atma

25　　"It is not easy — as I said, Arjuna — to fathom this mysterious concept of the True Self. Everything else in the world changes. Every creature, rock, blade of grass, human being, element, or component of any kind changes. Only the *Atma* never changes! Because it is never modified it is termed *immutable.* Because it is invisible, has no form, and cannot be heard, smelled, or touched, it is termed *unmanifested.* Because the human mind cannot perceive or conceive it, it is said to be *unknowable.* Why grieve over a Self that is immutable, unmanifested, and unknowable?"

26–27　　Krishna lets those ideas sink in, and then continues. "Even if you do choose to see yourself as a worldly body that dies, why suffer this anguish? Your despondency steals your strength. Death is inevitable for all the living. You know that death is certain in all of nature, so why mourn that which is natural? Nothing — absolutely nothing — in nature is permanent.

28　　"All beings are temporary. Before birth, they are unmanifested (nonmaterialized). At birth they become manifested. At their end they again become unmanifested. What is there in all this to grieve over? Grieving over the temporary just uses up your energy and holds back your spiritual growth.

29　　"No one really understands the *Atma,* Arjuna. One person sees it as wondrous, another speaks of its glory, others say it is strange, and there are many who listen but do not comprehend it at all. Very few even think of inquiring into what is beyond this physical world.

30　　"I am well aware that I have veered into high philosophy, but you must understand that all beings, whether called 'friend' or 'enemy,' have this indestructible *Atma* within. You must be poised above this debilitating sorrow of yours."

The Warrior's Personal Karma

"One's personal duty in life (one's *sva-dharma*) should be viewed as one's responsibility to his or her highest Self, the *Atma*. This ultrahigh level of duty carries with it the requirement that one *never* does anything that is contrary to this True Self Within. And even if you consider your *sva-dharma* more narrowly from the standpoint of being true to your profession, you should not hesitate to fight. For a warrior, war against evil, greed, cruelty, hate, and jealousy is the highest duty. 31

"The tide of fortune comes in but rarely. This war is a great, unsolicited opportunity for you to fight for righteousness; for a warrior this is no less than a free pass to heaven. Therefore, rejoice, Arjuna. Be happy. This is your opportune moment! 32

"But if you do not fight this battle of good over evil, you will fail in both your worldly duty and in your duty to your very Self. You will violate your *sva-dharma*. Not doing the right thing when it is required is worse than doing the wrong thing. 33

"If you do not do your duty the tale of your dishonor will be repeated endlessly. For a man of honor to go down in history as dishonorable is a fate worse than death. Ordinary human beings naturally strive to preserve their lives, but the warrior has a different way. Warriors must be ever ready not merely to safeguard, but to sacrifice their lives for a cause. Knowingly surrendering your life to an ideal increases your glory. 34

35   "But your superb soldiers will think it was fear that made you withdraw. Though they esteemed you before, they will treat you and your name with derision.

36   "Your enemies who have harbored a grudging respect for your prowess in battle will slander you and ridicule your bravery. Do you really think they will believe that you withdrew out of love for kith and kin? Those who used to shudder at the thought of fighting you will crack insolent jokes about your faintheartedness. Failure to do your duty will destroy the well-deserved reputation you built over many heroic battles.

37   "This battle is a righteous cause, Arjuna. No matter what happens, you win. If killed, you immediately enter heaven; if victorious, you achieve a great name and fame. Either way, you triumph. So, arise, Arjuna! Fight!

38   "And heed this important point about life in general: The way to win this great war is to react alike to both pain and pleasure, profit and loss, victory and defeat."

The Secret of Selfless Action

39   Krishna, as though to solidify that point, pauses a moment and then continues. "You have now heard an intellectual explanation of the principle of *Atma* (the True Self), and of the need to discriminate between the Real (unchanging) and the not-Real (*anything that changes*). Now pay attention while I explain a practical spiritual discipline called *karma yoga* for living a more effective, happier life in this vexing, ever-changing world. This is the path of selfless, God-dedicated action. By making this your path you can

live a spiritual life and yet stay fully active in the world. You can remain a man of action, achieving your very best, and yet not be bound or caught by the worldly.

"*Karma yoga* (literally, 'union with God through action') is not in the least bit dangerous, Old Friend. On this path no effort ever goes to waste and there is no failure. Even a little practice of this will protect you from the cycle of death and rebirth. 40

"When one's actions are not based on desire for personal reward, one can more easily steady the mind and direct it toward the *Atma,* the True Self Within. For the person of steady mind, Arjuna, there is always just one decision, but for the quivering mind pulled in a thousand directions, the decisions that plague it are endless, and they exhaust one's mental strength. People with an unsteady mind inevitably end up failing; those with an unwavering mind achieve great success. 41

"There are people, ignorant of this principle, who take delight in their own particular dogma, proclaiming there is nothing else. Their idea of 'heaven' is their own enjoyment. The main reason they do their activities is to achieve the pleasures and power that 'heaven' promises. Thus, even though their motive is common and positive, they are in truth filled with rather selfish desires. 42-43

"With their minds thus taken up by their own selfish desires for everlasting pleasure and power, they are not able to develop the utter concentration needed to reach union with God, which is mankind's only real objective. 44

"The scriptures describe three components of nature (called *gunas*). I will describe these in more detail later, 45 but for now, concentrate on transcending *all* of them. Focus on going beyond all of nature and all worldly attachments. To be bound to worldly nature is certainly not the purpose of life. Focus instead on the Eternal that lies beyond this worldliness. Concentrate on freeing yourself from the tyranny of the so-called pairs of opposites. Release yourself from always trying to evaluate and judge everything. Disentangle from your habit pattern of seeing things as good or bad, lovable or hateful, pleasant or painful, and so forth. The tendency to get trapped in apparent opposites is a common and debilitating malady. Instead, remain tranquil and centered in the Self (*Atma*). Take care not to seek acclaim or acquire earthly objects.

46   "A reservoir that is necessary during a dry spell is of little use during a flood. Similarly, to the enlightened person even scriptures are superfluous. Yes, live amicably with worldly existence, but know you must transcend it. Prepare yourself for nothing less than union with Divinity itself!

47   "Work hard in the world, Arjuna, but for work's sake only. You have every right to work but you should not crave the fruits of it. Although no one may deny you the outcomes of your efforts, you can, through determination, refuse to be attached to or affected by the results, whether favorable or unfavorable.

"The central points of issue, Arjuna, are desire and lack of inner peace. Desire for the fruits of one's actions brings worry about possible failure — the quivering mind I mentioned. When you are preoccupied with end results you pull yourself from the present into an imagined, usually fearful future. Then your anxiety robs your energy and, making matters worse, you lapse into inaction and laziness.

"One does not accomplish great ends in some by-and-by future, O Warrior. Only in the present can you hammer out real achievement. The worried mind tends to veer from the only real goal — realizing the *Atma,* uniting with Divinity, the True Self Within.

"The ideal, Arjuna, is to be intensely active and at the same time have no selfish motives, no thoughts of personal gain or loss. Duty uncontaminated by desire leads to inner peacefulness and increased effectiveness. *This* is the secret art of living a life of real achievement!

"To work without desire may seem impossible, but the way to do it is to substitute thoughts of Divinity for thoughts of desire. Do your work in this world with your heart fixed on the Divine instead of on outcomes. Do not worry about results. Be even tempered in success or failure. This mental evenness is what is meant by *yoga* (union with God). Indeed, equanimity is *yoga!* 48

"Work performed with anxiety about results is far inferior to work done in a state of calmness. Equanimity — the serene mental state free from likes and dislikes, attractions and repulsions — is truly *the ideal* attitude in which to live your life. To be in this state of mind is to be lodged in the Divine. Pitiful are those pulled by the fruits of their action. 49

"When you are endowed with this basic detachment, you shed the *karmic* consequences of both your good and bad deeds, casting aside the inevitable effects of your actions. Never lose sight of the overriding goal, which is to free yourself from bondage during this lifetime, to shed attachment to worldly things, detach from ego, and truly release yourself from the wheel of 50 birth and death. When you do this, you actually become one with God.

"I see that you sigh at this breathtaking goal, Arjuna. Know that you can achieve this by first uniting your heart with God and only then pursuing worldly things. Proceed in this order, not in the reverse order, and then your actions will be linked to the very purpose of life — which is, again, union with the Divine.

51   "A *yogi* is a truly wise person whose consciousness is unified with Brahman (the Godhead).* True *yogis* are detached. They are not at all concerned about the fruits of their actions and thus have left all anxiety behind. Detachment is the means to convert misery-laden *karma* (here indicating the entangling consequences of one's acts) into misery-free living. Detachment is the means for rising above worldly activities and getting to a state *beyond* the worldly.

"Achieve that transcendent state, Arjuna, and enter the battle not merely as a soldier but as a man of true wisdom, a *yogi*. These high spiritual teachings are not meant just for the recluse; they are intended for active people like you, immersed in the hustle and bustle of the world.

52   "When your mind crosses the mire of delusion and your intellect clears itself of its confusion about the truth of who you really are, your True Self, then you will become dispassionate about the results of all your actions.

---

* *Brahman,* the Godhead, is the Supreme, Divine Presence — the Absolute Highest Consciousness (not to be confused with *Brahma,* the Creator, or *Brahmin,* the priestly class).

"At present, Arjuna, your mind is bewildered by con- 53
flicting ideas and philosophies. When it can rest
steady and undistracted in contemplation of the True
Self Within, you will be enlightened and completely
united in love with the Divine. This is where *yoga*
reaches its culmination: the merging of individual
consciousness in Cosmic Consciousness. This is nothing less than the goal of life!"

Description of the Illumined Ones

Arjuna, listening attentively, interrupts. "But Krishna, 54
how does one identify the enlightened person you
describe, the one absorbed in the Divine? How would
such a one speak, sit, or move about, for example? If I
knew that I could better strive for it."

Krishna answers, "Old friend, you should strive to 55
become such a person! This person is called an Illumined One, a *Sthithaprajna* (literally, one who is
established in wisdom). This is the one who abandons
all selfish desires, cravings, and torments of the heart;
who is satisfied with the True Self (*Atma*) and wants
nothing outside the Self. This one knows that real
bliss is only found within.

"This is the man or woman whose mind is unper- 56
turbed by sorrow and adversity, who doesn't thirst for
pleasures, and is free of the three traits that most tar-
nish the mind — namely attachment, fear, and anger.
Such a one is an Illumined One, a *Sthithaprajna*.

"The person who is detached, desireless, who neither 57
rejoices nor gets depressed when faced with good fortune or bad — that person is poised in wisdom above
worldly turmoil and is therefore an Illumined One.

58   "The Illumined One has learned to deftly withdraw the senses from the attractions of the world, just as the turtle naturally pulls in its limbs to protect itself. This is very important, Arjuna. Let Me explain further.

59–60   "When people pull back from worldly pleasures their knowledge of the Divine grows, and this knowing causes the yearning for pleasure to gradually fade away. But inside, they may still hanker for pleasures. Even those minds that know the path can be dragged away from it by unruly senses.

"Much of one's spiritual discipline must therefore focus on taming wayward senses and being ever vigilant against the treacherousness of the senses. The refinement of an individual or a society is measured by the yardstick of how well greed and desires are controlled.

61   "The Illumined Ones subdue their senses and hold them in check by keeping their minds ever intent on achieving the overarching goal of union with God. They get in the habit of substituting Divine thoughts for attractions of the senses.

62–63   "The downward spiral to one's ruin consists of the following process: Brooding on (or merely thinking about) worldly attractions develops attachments to them. From attachments to sense objects come selfish desires. Thwarted desires cause anger to erupt. From anger arises delusion. This causes confusion of the mind and makes one forget the lessons of experience. Forgotten lessons of experience cloud the reason, which results in loss of discrimination (between Truth and non-Truth, Real and not-Real). Finally, losing the faculty of discrimination makes one veer from life's only purpose, achieving union with the Divinity within. Then, unfortunately, one's life itself is wasted.

"But when you can move about in a world that sur- 64–65 rounds you with sense attractions, and yet be free of either attachment or aversion to them, tranquillity comes and sits in your heart — and you are absorbed in the peace and wisdom of the Self within. Serenity, Arjuna, is the point at which all sorrow ends!

"This *Atmic* wisdom (knowledge of the True Self) is 66 not for all. Those with agitated, uncontrolled minds cannot even guess that the *Atma* is present here within. Without quietness, where is meditation? Without meditation, where is peace? Without peace, where is happiness?

"The roving mind that attaches to the objects of the 67–68 senses loses its discrimination and is adrift, a ship without a rudder. Even a small wind blows it off its safe-charted course. Those who use all their powers to restrain the senses, steady the mind, and free themselves from both attachment and aversion — they are the people of true wisdom, Illumined Ones.

"Worldly people perceive existence itself quite differ- 69 ently than do spiritually wise people. It is like night and day; what is nighttime for one is daytime for the other. What worldly persons experience as real — the body, earthly pursuits, pleasure, pain, illness, sensory attractions — the Illumined Ones see as not Real and of no consequence. What the Illumined One knows as Real — Spirit, quietness, and so forth — the un-enlightened consider to be unreal and of no value.

"Waters from many rivers continually flow into the 70 ocean but the ocean never overfills. In a like manner, desires and attachments constantly flow into the mind of the Illumined One, but he or she, like the ocean in its deepest depths, is totally still and never disturbed.

71   "To gain access to this state of utter peace, Arjuna, you must be free of ego (the sense of 'I' and 'mine'), and live devoid of cravings. You must forget desire.

72   "This is the fixed, still state of the Illumined One, the *Sthithaprajna,* the one firmly established in union with God. Once one achieves this state, one never falls back from it into delusion. Furthermore, the person in this state at the instant of death merges into Divinity and becomes one with the Divine. And this, Arjuna, as I have often repeated, is the very goal of life!"

CHAPTER 3

THE PATH OF ACTION
(*Karma Yoga*)

"Do your worldly duty, but without
any attachment to it or desire for its fruit.
Keep your mind always on the Divine....
Make it as automatic as your breath or heartbeat."

Arjuna interrupts, "O Krishna, you're adding to my confusion! You imply that knowledge is greater than action, but then you push me to fight this awful war. Well, fighting is action! Please be clearer: Which path, knowledge or action, is right for me — which one will without a doubt bring me to the supreme goal?"

Krishna replies, "Over the many good years that we have been as close as brothers I have not made this totally clear to you, but now I will. Know that at the very beginning it was I who laid out both spiritual paths: knowledge and action. I established the path of knowledge for the more contemplative person and the path of action for the busy, action-oriented person.

"Remember, Arjuna, true knowledge is knowing the *Atma*, the True Self Within. When you clarify your intellect through either contemplation or selfless action you get to realize the *Atma*. Both paths lead to realization of Self.

4-5 "Those who merely shirk worldly activities, thinking they are 'renouncing' action, cannot attain the Supreme goal. You first have to act. Mere refusal to act is futile. Even the supposedly 'passive' goal of clarifying the intellect and acquiring knowledge cannot be achieved without action. Look at nature. The fruit engaged in its task of ripening does not 'renounce' its task and sever its connection to the tree until it is fully ripe. Indeed, Arjuna, inaction, for even a moment, is impossible. Eating, sleeping, breathing, the heartbeat, even subconscious mental activities — all are actions. Everyone is helplessly driven to action by their own nature and by nature itself. Action is inherent throughout nature. From the single whirling atom up to the entire universe, all is movement, action.

6 "If one sits motionless but with one's mind ever thinking of sense attractions, that too is engaging in action. If you think that merely being motionless is being actionless, you are being a hypocrite and deluding yourself.

7 "Engage in action, do your work, but with full control of your mind and senses. And be aware that the work you do should contribute in some way, directly or indirectly, to the higher good of humanity.

8 "One is obligated to work, to act, even to maintain one's body — bathing, eating, sleeping, breathing. So

do your obligated duties, Arjuna. Duty-bound action is far better than inaction."

The Law of Sacrifice

"Action (*karma*) normally ties the human being to the wheel of birth and death, but not when performed as an act of sacrifice — not when the person offers up both the action and the fruits of the action to Divinity. Then, the action is nonbinding. One's job in life is to act selflessly, even sacramentally, without thinking of personal benefit. It is very possible for you to make great moral and spiritual progress in worldly life through action and yet not become fastened to the negative consequences of your actions.

"In the beginning, when I created the world, I set in motion the principle of sacrifice, saying, 'It is through *sacrifice* that thou shalt prosper and propagate.' My word 'sacrifice' is in no way associated with the common image of self-neglect or self-flagellation. *Sacrifice* is used here in a very special way: it means offering, helping, and being dedicated to the welfare of all humanity. It implies a mutuality of existence with all other beings. *Sacrifice* in this spiritual meaning of the word is a universal rule, a fundamental law of nature; *sacrifice* as the spirit of giving, which permeates all of creation. This *sacrifice* is a way for mankind to convert earthly misery into happiness.

"Worship, for example (also a misinterpreted word, which means honoring and revering), is a meaningful form of *sacrifice* as I use the term. Therefore, Arjuna, revere and honor (worship) the *devas*, the Divine entities, subtle powers of nature that dwell in sacrifice. Cherish them and they will cherish you. This mutuality is good for all humanity.

12   "Dear old friend, you should strike a balance in life between giving and getting. When you engage in selfless service (which is *sacrifice*), your desires are fulfilled, unasked, by nature. Righteous people give more than they receive; indebted ones get more than they give. The one who receives without giving is stealing.

13   "You should even eat your food in the spirit of sacrifice. Then you are freed from the strong attachment to tastiness and enjoyment that so quickly binds one to physical gratification, which is a bottomless pit. The person who eats solely for physical enjoyment gets turned away from life's true purpose: achieving Divinity. Indeed, the very definition of *sin* is not, as so many think, committing evil acts, but veering from God. In that sense, eating merely for physical pleasure is a sin.

14   "The very cycle of life emanates from the subtle effects of *sacrifice* as here defined. Let Me explain the cycle: all living creatures are nourished and sustained by food; food is nourished and sustained by rain; rain, the water of life, emanates from nature, called down from heaven, freely given (*sacrificed*) for the eventual benefit of humanity. All of life, Arjuna, is therefore born of, nourished, and sustained by selfless action, by sacrifice.

"Sacrifice is the noblest form of action. Work performed in the right attitude of mind becomes sacrifice. Service is sacrifice. This level of sacrifice actually has Divinity in it, performing it becomes a subtle but powerful mental force. This makes life itself sacred. Eventually, all your actions, mental and physical, become an offering (a sacrifice) for the betterment of the universe.

15   "As I said, every selfless, sacred action (every sacrifice) is born from Brahman, the Godhead, the Absolute

Highest Consciousness. He is present, consciously, in every act of service. Work performed with the best of motives becomes sacrifice. Life itself is turned into a sacrifice when directed to the service of Divinity. When people perform service as sacrifice, no matter what their work or profession, the universe itself becomes elevated and sublime. The whole scheme of nature is centered not on grabbing, but on offering selfless action, which is sacrifice.

"This important law of life may seem distant from the individual, Arjuna, but that is not so. Each selfless act done by anyone contributes in an important way to this mysterious whole.

"All life turns on this law of sacrifice, called 'the wheel   16
of *yajna.*' Those who veer from this and seek instead to indulge the senses for personal gratification and ignore the needs of others, live in vain and squander their life. Why did I, the Creator, set this in motion? Because this world is a learning ground, a place to discipline, train, and elevate all beings. If we decline to learn we cannot derive the benefit of the schooling."

The Self (Atma) Is Beyond Karma

"Arjuna, those who have found the pure contentment,   17
satisfaction, and peace of the *Atma* (the True Self Within) are fulfilled. They have nothing more in this world to accomplish, no more obligations to meet. Being in the *Atma,* these people are beyond karma.

"The one who is firmly established in the *Atma* knows   18
the real meaning of being *Self*-sufficient. That person has no dependence of any kind on anybody and has nothing to gain or lose by either action or inaction."

Work as God Works

19   "The point, old friend — and this is very important
      — is to do your worldly duty, but do it without any
      attachment to it or desire for its fruits. Keep your
      mind always on the Divine (*Atma,* the Self). Make it
      as automatic as your breath or heartbeat. This is the
      way to reach the supreme goal, which is to merge into
      God.

20   "There have been many who have done this. The
      renowned King Janaka (an ancient *karma-yogi*)
      attained union with God by performing worldly
      duties in this spirit. The ignorant cannot lead the
      community, Arjuna; it is the enlightened who are the
      best servants of society. So do your worldly work
      without attachment and for the best interests of all.

21   "Whatever a great man or woman does, others also
      do. Eminent people must in the public interest put
      forth their best virtues. Then ordinary people try to
      rise to that level.

22–24 "Consider Me, Arjuna. There is nothing I do not have,
      so I have nothing to gain in this or the other worlds.
      And yet I continue doing. If I, Divinity, were to stop
      working, humanity would follow that example and
      this would inflict havoc. Indeed, if I cease to act it
      would cause cosmic chaos and result in confusion and
      the destruction of humanity.

25   "The people who are ignorant of the True Self Within
      work as though tightly harnessed to action, working
      for their own welfare. But enlightened persons who
      know the True Self work for the welfare of the world,
      unattached, ever helping to point humanity toward
      dharma (right action, living a truth-based life).

"And yet, do not bewilder the ignorant who are hun-   26
gry for selfish action. Let them continue to work, but
show them by example that work can be made sacred
when done in the right spirit, with the heart fixed on
Divinity.

"The ignorant one, mistakenly identifying with the   27
body, erroneously thinks, 'I am the doer.' This is the
mark of egoism. In truth, Arjuna, all actions are really
performed by worldly nature, not by *Atma*. The Self
(*Atma*), remember, is beyond all action, all *karma*.

"The person who really knows nature — which I will   28
explain to you in detail later — knows that when the
senses, which are a part of nature, attach themselves to
worldly objects, which are also a part of nature, it is
merely nature attaching to nature. It is only 'I,' this
ego-self, doing this or that. The wise one, aware of
this, stands apart and just watches this play of nature.

"The wise ones who understand these things should   29
not refrain from action, as that would confuse the
minds of the unknowing who are entangled in and
tied to the consequences of action (*karma*). There is
no harm in some people performing their duties with
attachment; work with attachment has its place in
humanity's evolution."

Transmuting One's Own Nature

"Now that you are aware of the indispensable neces-   30
sity of performing action, I will tell you the best path
for you, old friend. Shake off this fever of ignorance
that has enveloped you. Break free of your ego. Stop
thinking of worldly rewards. Fix your mind in Me, the
Truth, your *Atma*, the Divinity within you. Know

that it is the Divine who propels all actions in the universe. Offer up all your actions to Me, Divinity. And then, with a perfectly clear mind and heart, go forth, fight this battle of life!

31   "There are marvelous benefits from this selfless way of life, Arjuna, but you cannot acquire them without firm faith. These principles must be lived, not intellectualized. Those who earnestly live them are released from their *karma,* the consequences of their actions.

32   "But those who carp about these teachings and do not practice them are deluded and without spiritual discrimination. They are the cause of their own sorrow and ruin, and become lost.

33   "All living creatures, even wise sages, behave in accordance with their own nature. This is an important point. Everyone's behavior is rooted in the thoughts and the tendencies that predominate in them. This is the meaning of one's 'nature.' Therefore, if one's nature is so powerful, one might well question the value of even attempting to live by the scriptural injunctions to 'do this, don't do that.' One could ask: 'Why, if we are but pawns of our nature, should we even try to restrain it?'

34   "The answer is not to try to restrain your nature but to progressively improve your nature. Examine this thing called 'nature' more closely. One's own senses are major stumbling blocks to spiritual attainment. Senses derive their power from the many likes and dislikes imprinted in the mind (by family, by culture, and by one's actions in this and previous lives). This deeply embedded, largely unconscious system of likes and dislikes is what gives rise to one's thoughts,

desires, and tendencies. This mental pattern is in large part what is meant by one's 'nature.'

"Arjuna, the best thing to do with these thoughts and desires is to transmute them into a devotional attitude, a desire for God. When this attitude takes hold, the system of likes and dislikes melts away, which causes the fierce power of the senses to gradually dry up. Desires are enemies when directed outward, but allies when pointed inward toward Divinity.

"Remember, Arjuna, that life in the body and senses is not an end in itself, but only a passing phase. Truly, if the eye does not help one visualize God in everything it sees, it is better to be blind. If the ear drags one into filthy cacophony, it is better to be deaf. The senses should not be instruments that plunge you into muck; they should serve your interests, control your appetites, and help you dwell in Divinity.

"And do not think, Arjuna, old comrade, that it would 35
be easier to abandon your present responsibilities. One's duty in life is one's *dharma*. This essentially means that you have to live by your inner Truth rather than your selfish desires. One must do one's duty. No matter how devoid of merit your responsibilities and commitments may seem, they are preferable to the responsibilities of another, no matter how well you may perform them. You, Arjuna, are a warrior-prince by birth and training. If you now try to avoid your duty and mutate into a *sanyasi* (spiritual ascetic) merely because you face doing some things that you imagine are painful, you will be violating your inner Truth (your conscience, your *dharma*), which is the root basis of your life! It is even better to die doing one's own duty than attempt to do the duty of another."

The War Against Anger and Desire

36　Arjuna's head droops, and then he asks, "What is this awful force that drags us even against our will into selfish deeds?"

37　Krishna replies: "That awful force is *desire*. Desire is the force that drags you — selfish desire, which rises from your action-oriented nature. Selfish desires are insatiable; the more you feed them the more they crave. That is what I meant by 'bottomless pit.' Desires never say, 'Enough.' And anger is always linked with desires, and anger corrupts everything. This desire-anger duo is your direst, most formidable enemy here on earth.

38　"Desires cloud your spiritual light and bury your power of discrimination. As a flame is covered by smoke, and a mirror is covered with dust, and an embryo hidden in the womb, true knowledge is concealed by desire. For spiritually advanced people, desire is like smoke and is easily blown away to reveal the light of knowledge. For worldly-caught people desire is more like dust that requires vigorous wiping so the light can shine. For really dull persons desire so enfolds them they are like an embryo buried in darkness; only time and a new birth will bring light. Note, Arjuna, that in all these levels of spiritual attainment it is desire that shrouds the glow of one's True Self Within.

39　"Greed is but desire swollen to grotesque size. The wise one knows that desire is the eternal, insatiable archenemy, and tries to steer clear of it. But despite one's best efforts, desire still puts on many disguises and sneaks furtively into the heart and mind.

"The key bastions of this fiercely destructive enemy   40
have to be found out before you can lay siege to them.
Marauding desire has captured, and now firmly occupies, all three bodily stations: the senses, the mind,
and the intellect. From these three field headquarters
desire attacks and kills wisdom and discrimination,
and shrouds the *Atma* within.

"Therefore, Arjuna, O fond friend and greatest of   41
warriors, attack these marauders, these desires. Recap-
ture your senses, mind, and intellect (higher mind,
buddhi, which we will deal with later) and use them
for Divine purposes. When you kill desire the splendor of *Atma* will shine.

"And know the strategic positions you should occupy   42
in this war. Desire holds more firmly to the subtle (the
more refined and difficult to notice) than to the gross.
The senses are more subtle than the body; the mind
more subtle than the senses; and the intellect more
subtle than the mind. Far above all is the *Atma,* subtlest of all, which is beyond any and all desire.

"Therefore, Arjuna, realizing the truth of your True   43
Self (*Atma*) is your principal weapon for eradicating
desire. Self-realization is the true spiritual knowledge
(called *jnana*). This level of knowing is beyond all
your lower qualities, no matter how fine, including
your mind and even your intellect. Let your very
highest Self, your true nature, rule. Control your self
with your Self."

CHAPTER 4

INTEGRATING KNOWLEDGE, ACTION, AND RENUNCIATION
(*Jnana-Karma-Sanyasa Yoga*)

"Whatever path a person travels to Me is My path....
All paths lead to Me."

Krishna then says, "I taught these same eternal truths to   1
Surya (the Sun God), Arjuna. He passed them on to his
son Manu, the very earliest man, and he to his son Iksh-
vaku, who was the first king, so that he could better
handle his worldly duties.

"Handed down in this way through the ages, eminent   2–3
sages learned these great secrets. But through time, the
right type of people became scarce, and the practice of
this knowledge dwindled. I use the word *secrets* not
because these truths are hidden but because so few
people are prepared to hear them today. I'm giving these

truths to you now, Arjuna, because I love you and you are worthy to receive this grace."

4   Arjuna looks puzzled, and interrupts, "But Krishna, how can a modern man instruct an ancient one? We have been close friends for many, many years, and I love you dearly, Krishna, but you are only five or six years older than I am. You were born ages, eons after Surya and those others. They are from a past so distant it is beyond imagination. Why do you say it was *you* who taught this in the beginning? And please don't just tell me it was you in an earlier life! That makes it even more strange."

5   Krishna laughs within Himself, knowing the right moment has come. "Arjuna," He says, "people say the sun rises and sets, but it does not 'rise' or 'set,' it is merely out of their sight. I am like that. I am not born nor do I die, but ordinary mortals, seeing me 'coming' and 'going,' think that I am born many times. For the sake of simplicity, let me say that you and I have both passed through many, many births. In this present lifetime you have forgotten them while I remember them all. I am aware of the continuity of My existence as *Atma* down through the countless ages, but you are unaware of your *Atma,* your lasting reality. That is the difference between us."

Krishna's Declaration

6   "And know also, Arjuna, that as the Divinity in all creatures and all of nature, I am birthless and deathless. And yet, from time to time I manifest Myself in worldly form and live what seems an earthly life. I may appear human but that is only My *maya* (power of illusion), because in truth I am beyond humankind; I just consort with nature, which is Mine.

"Whenever goodness and *dharma* (right action) weaken 7–8
and evil grows stronger, I make Myself a body. I do
this to uplift and transform society, reestablish the
balance of goodness over wickedness, explain the sublime plan and purpose of life, and serve as the model
for others to follow. I come age after age in times of
spiritual and moral crisis for this purpose.

"Strange? Yes. It is difficult for most people to com- 9
prehend that the Supreme Divinity is actually moving
about in human form. But for those few who dare to
learn the secret that it is I, Divinity, who is the Oper-
ator within them, their own Self, My coming in
human form is a rare opportunity to free themselves
from the erroneous belief that they are their bodies.

"Thus freed from this delusion these special ones 10
seek refuge in Me, the *Atma*. They become absorbed
in Me, always thinking and remembering the Divinity within themselves. Purified of their selfishness,
fear, and anger by the fire of this great knowledge,
they, as many before them, reach the Supreme goal.
For all intents and purposes these special ones
become one with Me. This is absolutely true; give up
any doubts.

"You may think this is partiality, but I have no 11
favorites. Whatever path a person travels to Me is
My path. In whatever way a person approaches Me,
I return like for like. If they treat Me as father or
mother, I treat them as My children. If they serve Me
as master, I accept their services as their Lord. If they
worship Me as a child, I approach them as a child.
Those who pine for Me, I pine for. To those who see
Me as friend I am friend. Even for those who perceive
Me as enemy I approach as an enemy. All paths lead
to Me, Divinity.

12   "Most who long for success in worldly pursuits pray
       to the gods (the minor deities) that their needs be ful-
       filled. In truth, any desire is a form of prayer, and
       often results in quick success. The higher the ideal,
       however, the more arduously one has to pursue it and
       the longer one must wait.

13   "In the beginning, I established the evolutionary
       system in nature whereby beings evolve toward spiri-
       tual perfection. I then established four groupings of
       people for the harmonious working of societies and
       the progress of humankind. These classifications
       correspond to progressively higher levels of con-
       sciousness and moral and spiritual attainment. All
       societies have generally similar groupings. The sys-
       tem sometimes unfortunately veers from its proper
       course, but know that the basic pattern is valid
       for the social harmony and clarity of purpose in all
       societies.

       "And know, Arjuna, that although people are, at their
       core, all one, there are differences within them based
       on their *karma* (the consequences of their previous
       actions), and based on their natural makeup. And
       know that even though I am the author of these dis-
       tinctions, I (the *Atma* within) am untouched by them
       because I am beyond all *karmas,* all consequences of
       My actions."

Freedom from the Wheel of Karma

14   "*Karmas* do not cling to Me (*Atma*) because, as I
       mentioned, I am not concerned with the fruits of My
       actions. Anyone who really understands this principle
       of *Atma,* the True Self Within, is likewise not bound
       by the consequences of their own actions.

"This is not a new discovery. The ancient seekers of   15
liberation were well aware of it. They carried out all
their worldly actions without any sense of ego, incurring no *karmic* consequences. Do the same, Arjuna.

"But even great sages sometimes were perplexed as to   16–17
what is action and what is inaction. I will tell you
which actions (*karmas*) you should perform and which
ones to avoid. This secret can actually free you from
the wheel of death and rebirth.

"The truly wise person (the *jnani,* the *yogi,* the   18
Sthithaprajna, or Illumined One) is the one who recognizes inaction in action, and action in inaction. He
or she sees that where there is apparent action taking
place at the worldly level, there may be true inaction
within the individual; likewise, where there is no
apparent worldly action taking place, there may be
considerable action occurring on the inner level.

"Arjuna, truly wise persons are in the world but not of
it. They may be very busy with earthly matters but
their heads and hearts stay in solitude. They are connected in this way to the *Atma* within. These are the
wise ones untouched by *karma.*

"Those who are ignorant of the True Self, thinking
instead that they are the body and the doer, may
attempt to renounce worldly actions, but at the inner
level they still have the turmoil resulting from their
attachments and desires. That inner turmoil is itself
action, and thus they are still incurring *karmic* consequences even while supposedly not acting.

"The truly wise act without scheming for the fruits of   19
their actions, and are therefore without inner turmoil.

This breaks the chain of *karma*. All their selfish desires have been consumed in the fire of knowing that they are not the body or the doer, but are indeed the *Atma*, the True Self Within.

20   "These ideas are new to you, dear friend, so listen closely. The wise ones I have been describing are ever-content and need nothing. They have abandoned all external supports. This is true personal freedom. They act, but to them the actions are adorations of Divinity. Disentanglement from desire for the fruits of their actions is the key to their success.

21   "Expecting nothing, hoping for nothing, abandoning everything, they keep the mind and senses under control. Having conquered desire they incur no negative *karma* even while acting in the world.

22   "These wise ones have transcended the pairs of opposites; they are the same in success or failure, indifferent to loss or gain; they never bother to compete or compare, are free of envy, and contentedly shoulder whatever comes to them. They too are not bound by *karmic* consequences even though performing worldly actions.

23   "All your *karma* melts away when you are unattached, when your mind is purified in the knowledge that all life is one, and when you perform your duties in the spirit of sacrifice as an act of devotion, an offering."

The Various Attitudes of Worship

24   "Arjuna, *everything*, every thing in creation is the Godhead! What is being offered is Brahman; the very act of offering is also Brahman; the one who offers is Brahman; even the fire into which the offering is

poured is Brahman. God is not distant, but is within yourself and is your Self. See Divinity in all your actions and you can actually achieve Union with the Godhead, Brahman. To do so requires being fully absorbed in Brahman, being constantly aware of Divinity every moment. No matter what you may be doing, whether eating, sleeping, working, praying, or breathing, this attitude of worship (which, remember, is *sacrifice*) aids the development of true knowledge and wisdom.

"Some aspirants offer worship to the minor gods.   25
When performed with true devotion these offerings bring spiritual growth. More evolved seekers fully dedicate themselves to the highest Godhead, Brahman, surrendering their individual consciousness to the Cosmic Consciousness — offering up their ego to the Lord.

"Some advanced aspirants actually learn to suspend   26
the physical senses of hearing, sight, taste, touch, and smell — offering them into the fire of sense restraint. In this way they control the stimuli at the gate before these enter their perception. Others do the opposite — not restraining the sensations before they enter, but controlling the *influence* of them on the mind itself. Both approaches produce the same result: purification of the mind, which is absolutely necessary for Self-knowledge.

"Others who are deeply knowledgeable (of the True   27
Self Within), in rare acts of worship offer up all their actions and all the activities of their senses, and even the functions of life energy, their heartbeat and breathing. Their minds become suspended, the objective world is negated, ego vanishes. At these times, ego stripped, the Self is so fully identified with *Atma* —

which is the personalized version of Brahman — that the performer of this sacrifice actually merges into Brahman.

28   "There are yet others whose way of worship is to offer up wealth and possessions. Still others offer up self-denial, suffering, and austerities (purifications). Others take clerical or monastic vows, offering up knowledge of the scriptures. Some others make their meditation itself an offering.

29   "Some offer up *prana,* the mysterious vital energy force within them. They do this through control of the breath, literally stopping their inhaling and exhaling.

30   "Yet others abstain from food and practice sacrifice by spiritualizing their vital energy — that is, by figuratively pouring their own vital life force into the Cosmic Life Force. The whole point of all these various methods of sacrifice (worship) is to develop a certain mental attitude. Those who live with a truly worshipful attitude, whose whole lives are offered up for improvement of the world, incur no sin (no *karmic* debt).

31   "This world is not for the person who performs no sacrifice, no worship. But those who actually live their lives as an offering partake of the nectar of God. Through selflessness they reach the Divine.

32   "Thus, as you can see, Arjuna, many and various are the offerings that people spread before God. All of them spring from the workings of the mind, senses, and body. Although action in its ordinary form is binding, when converted into worship (devotion) it is liberating. To be devotional is the sacred plan of nature.

"Offering up knowledge (spiritual knowledge of True   33
Self, and so forth) as a sacrifice is better than any material offering. The goal of all your work, all actions, is
not to multiply your possessions beyond proportions
(which only makes you earthbound), but to bring you
to spiritual wisdom (*jnana*), intuitive knowledge of the
True Self Within. You are alive solely to become
enlightened and united with God.

"Another good attitude that aids the development of   34
spiritual knowledge is to wholeheartedly revere someone who has genuinely achieved it. When one sincerely strives for spiritual enlightenment, Divinity in
some way puts one in contact with an enlightened
teacher. Sincerely question that teacher. As a burning
candle can light many others, an illumined soul can
bring light to many a competent inquirer.

"Arjuna, once you gain spiritual wisdom you will   35
never again be deluded or confused. You will see all of
creation in your True Self, and in Me."

The Power of Self-Knowing

"Spiritual knowledge (*jnana*) does what nothing else   36
can do. Even the foulest of misguided persons can sail
across the treacherous river of sin on the raft of this
special knowledge.

"Like a blazing fire, knowledge of True Self Within   37
reduces all three *karmas* to ashes: distant-future
karma, near-future *karma,* and current *karma*
(*prarabdha*), which is the *karma* that is presently
working itself out. This *Atmic* knowledge destroys the
first two *karmas* and renders the third type ineffective
even as it operates.

38   "In all the world, nothing purifies like spiritual knowledge (knowing the Self). But it takes searching inquiries into the nature of the Real and not-Real, and giving one's mind wholly to it. In due time one comes to know these things in one's heart.

39   "Hold spiritual wisdom as your highest goal, Arjuna. Make your faith deep. Restrain your senses. Then you will arrive at this wisdom quickly and achieve the perfect peace of Divinity.

40   "The ignorant (uninformed about *Atma* and without faith) waste their lives. Through their disbelief they alienate themselves from the Self and thus from true unity with others. As miserable people, they cannot be happy either in this world or any world beyond.

41   "People who really know Divinity, who have renounced attachment to the fruits of their work by offering it to the Divine, who have used the sword of knowledge to cut to pieces their doubts regarding the truth of their *Atma* — no bonds can hold these people. Though they are ever occupied with action, *karma* cannot taint them.

42   "O Prince, your ignorance of your True Self Within is the cause of your present reluctance to act, just as the opposite of ignorance, Self-knowledge, would bring fearless action. So with the sword of wisdom sever the doubts in your heart. Arise, O best of men, take your stand. Be a warrior!"

CHAPTER 5

CONTEMPLATING THE GOAL
(*Sanyasa Yoga*)

"Knowing this, you come to the place where all paths meet, and you achieve lasting peace of mind."

Arjuna blurts out: "I've been listening carefully Krishna, but one moment you recommend the path of knowledge or contemplation (a sort of *sanyasa yoga*), and the next moment, the path of desireless action (*karma yoga*). These seem to conflict. Which one is definitely better for me?"

Krishna replies, "Both paths lead to the same goal, which is liberation (*moksha*). But *karma yoga,* the action path, is better for you, Arjuna, and for most people. Many spiritual seekers assume they should withdraw like a *sanyasi* (renunciate), and they may for a time be blessed with tranquillity, but most often it is merely the ego masquerading as quietism.

3   "The person of selfless action (*karma-yogi*) who feels neither desire nor aversion and does not yearn for one thing or loathe another is the true 'renunciate.' What matters is not what you call yourself, but whether you escape your self-will (ego). With no ego you break free of *karma*.

4   "The uninformed think these two paths — renunciation (*sanyasa yoga*) and action (*karma yoga*) — lead to different results, but that is not true. They are essentially the same; compare them.

5   "Right knowing (*jnana yoga*) leads to right doing. Right doing (*karma yoga*) gives rise to right knowing. Take either path to the very end and they meet. At that place the contemplative seeker of knowledge greets the person of action, and they are both equally free from the cycle of birth and death. The person who knows this oneness of paths really knows the Truth."

The Role of Action (Karma)

6–7   "As I mentioned earlier, Arjuna, you cannot renounce action without first performing it. The *karma-yogi* comes to realize through the direct experience of selfless action in the world that life beyond the pull of worldly desire is better than life entangled in it. Without direct experience one has to rely on theory and concepts. Theorizing and make-believe have no place in one's spiritual career.

"The mind absorbed in the Divine even while engaging in earthly activities gets purified. Purifying your mind means that your sense of doership vanishes and God becomes the doer. It also means that you realize your Self as the *Atma* in all beings. This purity of mind and heart leads to higher spiritual discipline and thus to true oneness with the Godhead. It is at this highest of high places where the paths of renunciation and action converge.

"The enlightened person always thinks, 'I (the Real I) do nothing; I (this body 'I') am but the instrument.' He or she is constantly aware of this while seeing or hearing, touching or smelling, eating, moving about, sleeping, breathing, speaking, letting go or holding on, or even when opening or closing the eyes — aware that all these activities are but interactions among bodily senses and worldly objects. The activities may seem real but it is not the Self, it is merely nature at work. All actions pertaining to bodily existence take place in the worldly self, which is not the real Self. *Atma,* as you have learned, is beyond all worldly matters. 8-9

"As the lotus floating on the surface of muddy water stays untouched by the water, when you offer all actions to the Divine and surrender any yearning for the results, you cannot be tainted. 10

"Purity of action, mind, and heart is absolutely essential for further spiritual growth. To a *karma-yogi* who has turned his or her whole life toward Divinity, the body, senses, and intellect are just instruments for self-purification. Any work this *karma-yogi* performs is done dispassionately, and this enhances spiritual unfolding. 11

"The *karma-yogi* offers all works and all desires for the fruits of works to the Divine — and thus wins eternal peace in the Divine. But the person impelled by selfish desire gets entangled in agitations and anxieties of the mind. 12

13 "The true *yogi,* being a self-controlled person who has mentally cut free from worldly actions, lives content as the indweller, a mere resident in a body. These *yogis* do not incessantly drive themselves to act, nor do they involve others in action.

14 "It is mysterious, Arjuna. God established this system but does not operate it. Divinity does not determine the worldly doings of humanity, nor does It instill the sense of doership (ego) into humanity — nor even does It link actions to the consequences of actions. Nature does all this. All actions, all works, all *karma,* belong to nature, not the Divine. It is humanity that determines its earthly destiny. People seal their own fate.

15 "Further, God is neither responsible for nor takes note of anyone's bad or even good deeds. Both bad and good *karma* are the result of actions performed by people who mistakenly think that their True Self (*Atma*) is connected to the worldly — which it is not. This is an elusive but important point. The Divine is absolute perfection, poise, and bliss. Worldly acts have no place in this blessed purity. Thinking other-wise is what I mean by ignorance and delusion. I repeat: God, the True Self in each living being, is in no way a part of the goings on in worldly nature."

The Light of Wisdom

16 "As the darkness of night vanishes when the sun rises, so too the darkness of ignorance and delusion is dis-pelled when you gain knowledge of your True Self.

17 "*Jnana-yogis,* persons of wisdom (whom I previously referred to as *Sthithaprajnas,* Illumined Ones), cast out this ignorance of mind and thus erase past impurities.

They ever fix their purified minds on Divinity and stay completely absorbed in the Divine, their one and only goal. In this way they merge into God and are freed from the birth-death cycle, never to be born again.

"They know that sunlight falls equally on all crea- 18
tures. Those who possess this wisdom of Self look with a unified vision upon all beings and have equal love for all, whether those beings are spiritually advanced or the least in the ranks — or even a cow or a dog. The real knower of Brahman sees *only* Divinity everywhere, in every being and every thing.

"Even while in a body, these enlightened beings 19
(*jnana-yogis* or *jnanis*) transcend any notion of an existence separate from God. They continually focus their minds on the absolute oneness of Divinity, and on their own unity with That. Since the Divine is flawless, they are likewise without blemish or bias, reflecting God's utter perfection. This perfection is the same in all; it is called *Atma* — and yet, only the wise perceive it."

Attaining the Bliss of Brahman

"The wise ones, Arjuna, are totally free from delusion. 20
They know the Supreme Godhead (Brahman), and directly experience their own identity in That. They are neither elated by good fortune nor depressed by what is painful; they neither rejoice nor grieve. They know that the sensation called pleasure appears and disappears like a flash of lightning, and know that the cost of pleasure is inevitably misery and pain, which is indeed a dear price.

"These undeluded persons need no external sup- 21
ports whatsoever. Through intense meditation on the

Divine, fully absorbed in God, they have realized the eternal bliss that comes with living in the Self (*Atma*). With this spiritual awareness they rise above desire for sensory attractions and experience constant bliss. God intoxicated, they revel in Divinity and in nothing else.

22   "The wise recognize the transient nature of worldly gratification and thus do not look for happiness in the realm of the senses. Sensual delights are the wombs of misery. Earthly pleasures, though they seem enjoyable, are fleeting and ultimately painful. Wise ones know that misery inevitably, without fail, marches in lockstep with worldly pleasure.

23   "Desire and anger are counterparts, Arjuna. Anger is your response to the frustrations of unfilled desires. When you can control or transcend desire and anger (which arise in your body, not your *Atma*) you will have found true, lasting happiness.

24   "Those who find joy and peace completely within are the truly happy ones. Their bliss is in direct proportion to their disentanglement from worldly attractions. Eventually, they actually become one with Divinity, the very Source of the bliss that resides inside.

25   "These wise ones' sins (errors) have been washed away. Their desires, and the anger and greed that always accompanies desires, have vanished. Their ignorance has disappeared, cast out by knowledge of the *Atma*. Their minds and hearts are firmly resident in the Divine, always seeking to contribute to the welfare of all. Those who attain the eternal bliss of Divinity are the real holy ones.

"Those who actually experience Divinity have severed   26
the chains of selfish desire. Through constant, intense
effort they have taken charge of their minds and bodies and are actually above desire, anger, and greed.
They now dwell in their True Self experiencing eternal bliss everywhere!

"The process for vanquishing the mind and senses   27–28
consists of shutting out the external world, focusing
one's gaze on the center of spiritual consciousness
between the eyebrows, and gradually equalizing the
in-going and out-going breath. Then, when the body,
mind, senses, and intellect are under control (without
desire, fear, and anger), realization of the constant
freedom and bliss within the Godhead comes.

"Ceaselessly think only of Me, Arjuna. Know that I,   29
the Godhead (Brahman), am the object of all worship
and the receiver of all offerings. Know that I am the
source of all and the friend of all beings everywhere.
Knowing this, you come to the place where all paths
meet, and you achieve lasting peace of mind."

CHAPTER 6

TAMING THE MIND AND SENSES
(*Dhyana Yoga*)

"... not simply to know God, but to literally become one with God! This is the profound plan and purpose of creation that is hidden from most people."

Krishna continues the dialogue: "The person who works in the world without needing or expecting a reward is both a *sanyasi* (true renunciate) and *karma-yogi* (action *yogi*). But the person who merely refrains from acting in the world is neither of these. You cannot just discard worldly duties, but must do them to the utmost extent of your human capacity for excellence. 1

"I repeat, Arjuna, nobody can really become one with the Godhead without leaving their desires behind and abandoning their attachment to the fruits of their actions. The paths of desireless action (*karma yoga*) and renunciation (*sanyasa*) may seem to be different from 2 one another but they are not. All spiritual growth is based on surrendering attachments and selfish motives.

3   "The path for those who are climbing to spiritual heights is selfless action (*karma yoga*). For those who have made the summit (union with God), deep serenity and absence of thought is their way.

4   "God cannot be perceived in the mental ferment of the worldly. You have to blot out thoughts of the world. When you are no longer attached to performing action and have eliminated any desires for worldly things, only then will you have climbed to the highest state of *yoga* (which again is union with Divinity).

5–6   "I must emphasize, Arjuna, that you have to lift yourself by your own efforts! You must not allow yourself to be demeaned by your ego-self. Know that the self can be both friend and foe — a friend when used to conquer the mind, senses, and body; a foe when it drags one into the mind, senses, and body. True Self (*Atma*) is the ally; the ego-mind self is the enemy.

7   "The serene person who is absorbed in God, living thus in peace, is the true renunciate. Maintaining an even mind in heat and cold, pleasure and pain, honor and disgrace marks the spiritually mature. Maintaining physical, mental, and intellectual balance no matter how difficult the challenge leads to permanent cheerfulness, which is the sure sign of a *yogi*. (Recall, a true *yogi* is not a spiritual recluse, but a godly person of discipline who lives fully in the world.)

8   "The person who knows the *Atma* has conquered the senses and is calm under all circumstances — that

person has climbed to the summit of human consciousness. That *yogi* considers a clod of mud, a stone, or a gold nugget with the same equal-mindedness. Worldly people pursue earthly things; godly ones pursue only the Divine.

"The *yogi* who looks with the same eye upon saints or sinners, relatives or strangers, friends or foes, wellwishers or even those wishing harm is indeed supreme." 9

The Method of Meditation

"To attain this godly state, Arjuna, you must become fully immersed in the True Self through the process called meditation (*dhyana yoga*). You have to control your mind, body, and senses and become free of possessions, expectations, desires, and greed. You must live alone, at least internally, in a quiet place. This inner discipline called meditation is imperative because it is the means for achieving lofty and necessary ends. 10

"The method of meditation includes locating a clean spot to sit, neither too high or low, covered with *kusha* grass, a deerskin, and a cloth, in that order.* Then, the meditator strives to still all thoughts and sensations. Thus cleansing the mind returns it to its original state, inviting God to enter. 11-12

"While meditating, sit up straight, keep your body still, and keep your eyes from wandering by gazing at the tip of your nose. Or close the eyes and focus on the center of spiritual consciousness between your eyebrows. Remain in perfect calmness with your thoughts fixed on Me, the Divine. 13-14

---

* Some details of the ancient methods have of course changed over the years, but the principles are the same.

15   "Through long concentration one's mind ceases its wandering. After some time one develops what is in essence a new sensory faculty known as *medhanadi,* an intuitive penetrating skill that makes knotty issues of life no longer problems. The *yogi* with his or her mind constantly on the Divine finds deep serenity, the zenith of Self-realization, and merges with Me.

16-17   "People who eat too much or too little or who sleep too much or too little will not succeed in meditation. Eat only food that does not heat up the body or excite the mind. When you balance and regulate your habits of eating, sleeping, working, and playing, then meditation dissolves sorrow and destroys mental pain."

The Yogi

18-19   "The mind has long been dissipated by worldly things and does not easily come under sway, Arjuna. But when one perfectly controls and fully withdraws the mind from selfish cravings, one is in *yoga,* union with Divinity. The mind of the *yogi,* totally focused on the True Self, is unwavering like the steady flame of a candle in a sheltered place.

20   "When the mind becomes still and quiet, the Self reveals itself. At these depths one experiences the joy and peace of complete fulfillment.

21-22   "When you dive deep into this infinite bliss of the Lord, which is above and beyond the senses, you never again wander from the innermost Truth. The goal and the means for reaching the goal become one and the same; life itself becomes a meditation.

23   "In this supreme state you desire nothing else whatsoever and cannot be shaken by any calamity. To be in

this mental state is to know the real meaning of *yoga* (union with God). Indeed, to achieve this state is to sever your contact with pain and surely bring an end to all your sorrow.

"Renounce all selfish desires, which are but products of the ego. Use your mind to curb all your senses. Rein in your restless and fidgety mind from wandering outside to seek stimulation and satisfaction. Turn it inward and train it to rest in God. Keep your attention anchored in the *Atma,* your True Self. Think of nothing else. Then, peace and quiet will gradually arise in you. 24–26

"The one who reposes in utter quiet with the Divine, cleansed of desires and passions, who knows the truth of *Atma,* rests in the Supreme bliss of Brahman. Constantly united with the Godhead, this *yogi's* bliss is eternal. 27–28

"Touched in this way by God, this *yogi* sees unity and the True Self (Divinity) everywhere, in every creature, in all creation. 29

"Those who see Me in everything and everything in Me, know the staggering truth that the Self in the individual is the Self in all. As they live in constant spiritual awareness, I am never out of their sight or lost to them — nor are they ever out of My sight or lost to Me. 30

"Those who are in this cosmic union with Me, worship Me (Brahman) in the hearts of all. Whatever their external way of living or status, as they have shifted from self to God they live their lives in Me — and thus each of their contacts with other beings is, inwardly, an adoration. 31

32   "These high *yogis* know with certainty that they are one with Brahman, and therefore one with the universe. Thus they experience the joys and sorrows felt by others as happening to the whole. This is the loftiest spiritual union. I regard these *yogis* as highest of all — "

33–34   Arjuna interrupts again: "It's impossible, Krishna! My mind is so restless, so turbulent I can't imagine ever being able to achieve the loftiness you're teaching. The human mind is a nursery of waywardness, so strong it can drag an elephant, full of stubborn desires for worldly things. Indeed, it's like a mule. If it doesn't get what it wants it turns petulant and scheming. My mind can never be caught; it never halts in one place. Trying to catch and tame it is like trying to restrain the wild wind."

35   Krishna breaks into a smile. "You know the nature of the mind, Arjuna. It is restless and hard to subdue, but it can be done. There are four main ways to do it: through regular practice, relentless inquiry, non-attachment, and firm faith. Let Me explain.

"Through regular practice (*abhyasa*) you can draw the mind away from worldly attractions and back into the *Atma*. As it becomes more interior it becomes calmer. Relentless inquiry into the Self (*vichara*) leads to knowledge of *Atma,* the True Self Within. Non-attachment (*vairagya*) results from self-inquiry and discrimination (*viveka*). When you actively turn your thoughts to all the bad consequences of the desires as they arise in you, the passion for them gradually dries up. As your passion diminishes, your mind comes under control. Firm, dedicated faith (*sraddha*) brings you the raw force of determination, will. All four methods are subsidiaries of the practice of meditation.

"Those who have no mastery over their ego will find it difficult to control the mind. But those who struggle hard by the correct means (relentless practice and nonattachment) will prevail over their wayward minds." 36

Krishna's Promise

Arjuna again interrupts, "What if one dies trying, Krishna? What happens to the imperfect *yogi* who may have faith but simply can't subdue his mind and therefore wanders from the path, loses sight of the goal, and then dies, foiled in the attempt? Will this *yogi* have failed in both worlds, this one and the hereafter, like the cloud that just dies in the sky, unable to fulfill its mission of dropping rain? Dispel this dark cloud of doubt in me, Krishna." 37–39

Krishna responds, "Spiritual work is never wasted. Fear not, my friend. One who does this good work will not come to a bad end in this world or any world beyond. You must know this profound truth, Arjuna: The one who strives for realization never comes to grief! 40

"According to the law of *karma*, souls reincarnate in environments befitting their spiritual attainments. Good people (even those who have veered from the spiritual path) go, when they die, to the heaven of those who do good deeds. They dwell there for a number of years and then take birth again, this time into a home that is pure and prosperous. A few of them will be born into a family that is spiritually advanced, but such births are difficult to obtain. When this happens, the good environment draws out their latent spirituality and leads them rapidly toward liberation. 41–43

44   "The ones born into the pure and prosperous houses have the opportunity at first to enjoy the relatively tame desires they held in their former bodies. But as soon as those pleasures are done they feel irresistibly drawn to spirituality by the force of the good habits they strove for in the previous life. Even those who showed only a faint interest, merely inquiring about spiritual matters, progress further than the ones who merely follow the rites and ceremonies of their belief systems unthinkingly, and thus stall their true spiritual advancement.

45   "Through constant spiritual effort over many lifetimes a person becomes purified of all desires and achieves the ultimate goal of becoming one with God. Being a *yogi* means that one is seriously on the path but not necessarily at the end of it. One is a *'yogi'* during the process of becoming and should persist birth after birth, until fit for merging with the Supreme Godhead.

46–47   "The *yogi* moving toward Divinity is deemed more highly evolved than ascetics who practice severe penance, higher than the learned ones who know the scriptures, and above the ritualists who perform their rites seeking favors. All of these are to some extent still entangled in desire. So be a *yogi*, Arjuna!

"Know that the true *yogi* has chosen a great yet attainable ideal in life: to turn Godward, to constantly and consciously move toward Divinity — to not simply know about God, but to know God in the fullest sense, to literally become one with the Divine!

"This is the profound plan and purpose of creation that is hidden from most people. Arjuna, be the one who gives Me his whole heart. That *yogi* will be My very own."

Part 2

THE
VERY NATURE
OF GOD

CHAPTER 7

BOTH KNOWING AND
EXPERIENCING DIVINITY
(*Jnana-Vijnana Yoga*)

*"I know every being past, present, and future,
but nobody knows Me completely."*

Krishna says, "Let Me be very clear, Arjuna. It may seem   1
impossible to you, but a mere human can indeed come
to know God — not merely *about* God, but to really
know God. Listen while I explain how to do that:
Through devoting your whole mind to Divinity (Me),
loving only Me, meditating on Me, and depending
wholly on Me as your only refuge, you will, without any
doubt, come to know Me in My entirety.

"For this, you will need both knowledge of Divinity   2
(*jnana*) and wisdom of Divinity (*vijnana*). I will give
these to you. The difference between them is this: one
learns knowledge through the senses and mind — that is,

through sight and thinking; one gains wisdom through direct grasp, through insight and intuition. Knowledge 'knows' it at an intellectual level; wisdom 'realizes' it fully and is able to apply it in daily living. Once you combine both of these there is nothing more you need to know in this world.

3   "Only one person in many thousands seeks full God-knowledge. And of these, only one in many thousands truly gains it. Despite these odds, it is the intent of God that all beings are, in the fullness of time, destined to reach this degree of perfection. The rare ones who do attain this level of knowing become indistinguishable from Divinity (Me), and thus achieve liberation."

The Essence of Divinity

4-5   "Listen closely and I will explain the essence of Divinity. First, know that I have two aspects, a lower and a higher. My lower self is the realm of nature (*prakriti*). According to the ancient system of knowing, this is comprised of eight basic components: earth, water, fire, air, ether (space), mind, intellect (higher mind, *buddhi*), and ego. Note that these basic components are arranged in ascending order from gross matter (physical and chemical elements) to the more subtle and refined: mind, intellect, and ego (which is the basic sense of being a physical self). And note that all eight of these components, even the very subtle ones, belong to *prakriti,* the cosmos, the world of nature.

"Beyond this world of nature I have a second, higher aspect that is distinct from all of nature and yet interacts with it. This is My spiritual realm (*Purusha*). *Purusha* is the life force, the source of consciousness in all beings, and the animator of all life. This mysterious power supports and sustains the entire universe.

"The commingling of these two realms, nature (which is inert matter) and spirit (which is life consciousness), is the womb of all beings. Life itself originates in this union of nature and spirit. The entire universe evolves from these two aspects of Me, and will finally dissolve into Me. 6

"I am Pure Consciousness, Arjuna, the underlying essence of all elements and beings. Nothing whatsoever exists separate from My Divinity. There is no power in the cosmos that does not emanate from Me and belong to Me. The entire universe is suspended from Me as if I were the string in a necklace of jewels. The gems may differ vastly, but the force holding them all together, the central thread, is Me, Divinity. 7

"I am the innate nature of everything. In pure water I am the sweet taste. In the sun and moon I am the radiance. In the very center of human beings I live as virility and courage. I am the sacred word *Om*, which designates the Divine, and I am the sound of it heard throughout the universe. 8

"I am the slight, delicate scent, the sweet fragrance of the earth. I am the brilliance in both fire and sun. I am the light of Divinity in all beings. I am the subtle spirit in spiritual practices that gives them their existence — I am the love in the devotee, for example, or the austerity in the ascetic, or the sweet sense of charity in the giver. 9

"I am the primordial seed of all entities, the power of discrimination (*buddhi*) in those who are intelligent, the splendor within all resplendent beings and things. 10

"Of the strong, I am their might and vigor. As I am beyond all attachments, I am the power in unselfish 11 desire. I am the subtle force in good actions that puts them in harmony with the welfare of humanity. I am the innate urge to help others."

Maya *and the* Gunas

12   "Arjuna, all of nature consists of three characteristics called *gunas*. The first is goodness (*sattva*), the second is passionate activity (*rajas*), the third is darkness, indolence, inertia (*tamas*). All these come from nature, which is My lower nature. I put on the appearance of this natural world but am separate from it. These three qualities of nature are contained within Me, Divinity, but I am not *in* them in the sense that I need to rely on them in any way. I do not rely on nature, it relies on Me.

13   "The three basic qualities of nature (goodness, passion, and darkness) are like the three primary colors, which combine in an infinite number of ways to create all hues in the universe. These *gunas* likewise combine endlessly to create all of the variety in nature. It all seems 'real,' but as it is constantly changing, it is not Real. Due to this *maya* mentality (the illusion that the world is Real), people do not look beyond the veil of illusion to Me, the unchanging consciousness, the Absolute Reality beyond all the worldly; they do not see beyond to Me, the very basis of it all.

14   "This curtain of illusion (*maya*) is hard to see through, Arjuna. Only those who love and depend completely on Divinity are eventually able to see through it.

15   "Those who are unable to see beyond the veil cannot, in effect, discriminate between Real and not-Real. Oblivious to the Reality of their own higher nature (the

True Self Within), they sink to their lower nature and do evil deeds, committing acts that turn them away from Divinity. Not knowing the holy from the unholy, they are of course not devoted to Me, Divinity."

The Four Devotees

"Four types of people seek a connection with Me: One, the world-weary — people who worship God for the alleviation of physical or mental agony, or to be released from fears and adversity; two, the seekers of happiness through worldly things — people who pray to God to obtain wealth, family, power, prestige, and so forth; three, the seekers of spiritual advancement — people whose motive for connecting with Divinity is to gain knowledge and experience to aid their self-realization; four, the wise — people who truly know the *Atma* (Self), who know that God alone exists, and whose only impulse is for the Divine and nothing else. 16

"Of these, the last is the highest because they know My Truth and are devoted to Me. As I am supremely dear to them, they are very dear to Me. The first three are attached to the worldly objects or mental states they desire. 17

"But certainly all four types are noble, because any reason for turning Godward will in due time lead to spiritual transformation and is therefore ultimately good. The wise ones of the last category, however, are My very Self. They know Me as the essence within themselves and are always with Me. Their devotion stands foremost. As fuel thrown into the fire becomes fire, the wise, absorbed in Me, actually become one with the Godhead, their own Divinity, their one and only goal. 18

19   "After many a long life of meditation on Me, these wise ones come to Me. They see that all this world is indeed their innermost Self, and realize that God alone puts on the appearance of all phenomena. Such great souls are rare indeed.

20   "Others, hoping to fulfill worldly desires, drift to lesser gods and offer rituals and rites. It is quite easy for them to get to those limited deities but the rewards are correspondingly small. Healing disease, winning litigation, acquiring a position, and other trifling psychic powers are alluring to worldly-caught people. True devotees of the Supreme Godhead give no thought to worldly things. The question of other gods does not even arise in them.

21   "And yet, Arjuna, whatever form of God people choose to worship in good faith, it is I, the Godhead, who makes their faith steady and unwavering. I do this to help them evolve stage by stage along their spiritual paths.

22   "Endowed with that steady faith, they get what they pray for. The objects they receive are, in reality, dispensed by Me. The needs of all beings are fulfilled only through Me, the Cosmic Source.

23   "The fruits they pray for, however, are ephemeral, perishable (and thus not Real), providing only fleeting satisfaction. Worshipers of these deities of the senses go to them; My devotees come to Me.

24–25   "People of little wisdom do not understand My supreme, immutable existence and thus they think of Me only as a finite figure, a worldly body. They are unable to grasp the transcendent Godhead beyond My human form. I do not reveal Myself to them. Very few can see through this veil of illusion called *maya* that I hold in front of Me.

"Arjuna, My delusive *maya* and I are always comingled. While others are deluded by the appearance of physical 'reality,' I am all-knowing. I know every being — past, present, and future — but nobody knows Me completely. If individual souls do not know their own Truth (*Atma*), how are they to know the truth of God, the Cosmic Soul?   26

"Why is it that people do not know this deep truth? Because as soon as they are born they are led to believe that the world around them is 'real.' They forget their oneness with Divinity and fall into a pattern of likes and dislikes that gives rise to all sorts of desires, attachments, and aversions. With their nervous systems thus conditioned, their sense of individuality (ego) is reinforced time and time again. It does not dawn on the impure mind preoccupied with ego to make room for devotion to God. Without that devotion it is impossible to see one's oneness with God.   27

"But those who purify their actions by dedicating them all to the Divine gradually grow less influenced by their own habits and desires. One step at a time, they overcome the lower self, worshiping Me, the One who is not separable.   28

"No matter how strongly you ascribe to the universal delusion that you can avoid pain and only have pleasure in this life (which is utterly impossible), sooner or later you must confront the fact of your inevitable aging and eventual death. Some people, trying to escape the fear of death, come to Me for refuge. Once with Me, they learn of their True Self (*Atma*) and ascertain the nature of Divinity. Therefore, because   29 death stirs people to seek answers to important spiritual questions, it becomes the greatest servant of humanity, rather than its most feared enemy.

30   "Finally, Arjuna, *yogis* know that it is I, the Godhead (Brahman), the *Adhyatma,* who presides over the entire cosmos, including the physical universe (*adhibhuta*), the deities who serve Divine purposes (*adhidaivas*), and the spirits who handle all sacrifices or offerings (*adhiyajna*).

"The wisdom and devotion of these *yogis,* these wise souls, serves them throughout their lives — and especially at the hour of death, the time when most people are scared and confused. That is why spiritual wisdom is so important. These *yogis* truly know their own *Atma* (which is Divinity itself, Me), and so they calmly accept death as a matter of course. Their God-realization is at its zenith when they drop their bodies. At that instant their whole consciousness becomes one with My Cosmic Consciousness, and they are thus liberated from rebirth."

CHAPTER 8

THE IMPERISHABLE GODHEAD
(*Akshara Brahma Yoga*)

*"The point is not to hope for a good birth
but to aim for a good death."*

Arjuna says, "Please wait a minute, Krishna. Your words   1–2
raise several questions in me: Just what precisely is Brahman, the Supreme Godhead, and what is this *Adhyatma*
you mentioned? And what is the essential nature of
karma? What, really, are those other things you referred
to — *adhibhuta, adhidaiva,* and *adhiyajna*? I know you
alluded to them as spirits or dieties who serve Divine
purposes, but what exactly do you mean? And how
exactly are *yogis* united with the Godhead at the time of
their death?"

Krishna obliges. "You have asked seven questions, Arjuna,   3
some of them rather abstract. Time is running fast, the

war faces us with open jaws, so listen closely. First, Brahman (the Godhead) is My absolute highest nature, vaster than whatever you call vast, omnipresent, immanent everywhere, the Imperishable (indestructible, undying, eternal) Divine.

"Next, the term *Atma* (or *Adhyatma*) is used to indicate the exact same vastness, the earliest Supreme Godhead existing in all individual beings. It cannot be known without great effort.

"Next, *karma* (here meaning action) refers in this context to My original vibrations, the initial actions that brought all creation into existence and keeps it going. (All beings are a part of this *karma*.)

4   "The prefix *adhi* means the 'beginning' or 'first,' the 'original.' It connects these terms directly with the all-pervasiveness of the primordial Godhead (Brahman). *Adhibhuta* pertains to the earliest, most initial Divinity that exists in the physical universe, and particularly in the elements and thoughts that comprise the individual. *Adhidaiva* refers to the primordial Divinity that dwells in the numerous lesser deities who, as My agents, operate an individual's body, mind, and senses. The eye is illumined by Surya the Sun god, the hand by Indra, and so forth. And the term *adhiyajna* refers to the earliest Divinity in the act of giving, the primordial spirit of selfless sacrifice that flows throughout creation.

"The point in all this is that Divinity is actually present throughout the universe, in every object, all creatures, and each individual being — and it always has been. Furthermore, this same Divinity exists within each and every activity that all these beings do in daily life — and it has been that way forever.

"Despite the fact that humanity finds numerous ways to separate God from the world, and despite the fact that everything in the world is perishable (including your body, I remind you), know that all of it is totally pervaded by the Imperishable Supreme Divine, which is Me."

How to Die

"Regarding your final question, which is very important, know this: whoever remembers Me at the time of death will no doubt come to Me. That person's consciousness will merge into My cosmic consciousness. 5–6

"This is a universal law, Arjuna. The sum total of all thoughts and feelings during the whole span of your life condense into a single state of mind at the time of your departure from the body. You assume a particular mental makeup at the instant of death. Whatever occupies your attention throughout life will inevitably be your consciousness at the moment you die — and to that realm of consciousness you will go. Then, some time later, that same mental structure is manifested back into the world. This is called the next birth.

"So what should you do? Throughout life, prepare for the death moment. Actually, the moment of death does not mean some future instant in time, it means this very moment! Any moment may be your last, so treat each as the last because your thought at that instant is the foundation on which your next birth is assembled. 7

"Live in a state of constant spiritual awareness. Do everything for God. Think of the Divine every minute.

Like the street musician who artfully plucks the guitar and at the same time plays the pipes fastened to it, do your earthly duties well, but simultaneously be aware at every moment of the Godhead. Do your duty, Arjuna, fight, but do it with your mind and heart fixed on Me. Then you will surely come to Me.

8   "The well-practiced mind does not wander after anything else. Through constant practice (*abhyasa yoga*) living becomes a lifelong meditation on the Divine. Then, no matter what you may be doing, you are imbibing godly tendencies. This becomes a habit of the mind. Educate your mind to this habit. This is how one finds God and goes to God.

9   "The Divine knows everything. The Divine is the intelligence behind the functioning of the entire cosmos, the Sovereign Ruler who designates the structure and working of the universe. The Divine is subtler than the subtle and yet the support of all; It is inconceivable, incomprehensible, as bright and unchanging as the sun, beyond the darkness of ignorance, above illusion. The Divine is the First Cause. Before Divinity there was nothing.

10   "Remember the Divine this way at the time of death. I cannot emphasize enough the importance of this. When it comes time to depart your body, still your mind completely; draw your life force utterly into the center of your spiritual awareness (between the eyebrows). In this way you will reach Divinity.

11   "I will now tell you of the supreme goal, the eternal state that is deathless, the imperishable, indestructible state that all scriptures point to, which is beyond death and rebirth. This state can be entered only by self-controlled people untainted by worldly desires.

"At the time of death, one should close down the gates   12–13
of the senses, place the mind in the shrine of the (spiritual) heart, focus all life-force energy upwards to the
center of consciousness between the eyebrows, and
repeat the syllable *Om,* which represents Me, Brahman, the Supreme Godhead.

"It is not just the outer sound of *Om* that is beneficial;
it is what happens inside. The act of vocalizing this
sound helps focus your thoughts single-pointedly on
the One, on God. When you are absorbed in repeating
this syllable, which is in essence the Divine name, you
are concentrating on the Divine — and then you will
achieve the supreme goal, Divinity. As the river enters
the ocean, your individual consciousness (*Atma*) flows
into the Cosmic Consciousness, Brahman.

"Arjuna, in a sense this is the very essence of My   14
teachings. The easy way to merge with Me, Brahman,
is to constantly, steadfastly, relentlessly remember Me
always, at every moment of your life! In this way you
are ever prepared for your end. One's next birth
depends on how one's death takes place. The point is
not to hope for a good birth but to aim for a good
death.

"This world is transitory and full of suffering. Those   15
great souls who have perfected their lives and come to
Me are no longer subject to rebirth into yet another
lifetime. Avoid birth and you avoid death."

The Planes of Existence

"The levels of existence beyond death are known   16
as the *lokas* (worlds). The highest among them is
Brahma-loka. All of these worlds and all the beings
that inhabit them, from *Brahma-loka* downward, are

subject to rebirth, including Brahma Himself (not Brahman — Brahma, the aspect of God that acts as the creator). But the one who climbs beyond these middle planes and reaches Me, the Absolute state, knows no rebirth.

"One gets what one is worthy of, Arjuna. Those who do not advance past the notion of heaven and hell commit themselves to the intermediate worlds and tie themselves to death and rebirth.

17–19 "Contemplate the cosmic standard of time and creation. When Brahma the creator wakes up at the dawn of each cosmic day, this entire universe and all creatures in it are instantly manifested, only to be dissolved back into the unmanifested (formless) at Brahma's cosmic nightfall. But each cosmic day and night of Brahma lasts thousands of *yugas,* and each *yuga* lasts 10,000 to 400,000 years; the time is all but incomprehensible to humans. In succeeding days and nights of Brahma, the same multitude of beings helplessly come to birth and death again and again as the physical universe continues its expanding and contracting.

"This eternal cosmic play is the same in the microcosm of the individual soul as it is in the cosmos. When an individual goes to sleep, the entire world his or her mind experiences as 'real' withdraws, only to 'come alive' again at waking."

Immortality

20 "But beyond even the mysterious, unmanifested state into which all beings dissolve at cosmic nightfall, there is another unmanifested reality. It is Brahman, the Godhead, the Thing-in-Itself that is beyond time, that does not perish even when existence itself dissolves!

"It is this eternal, absolute Thing-in-Itself that is the 21
ultimate goal. I am That, Arjuna. All those who come
to this ultimate home come to Me, never again to be
separate, never again to return.

"The only way to reach this immortal state is through 22
love, through unswerving devotion to Me (the
Divine) alone. As the individual wave does not have
any existence independent of the sea, the separate soul
does not have any real existence apart from Me, the
Universal Soul.

"There are two paths for the individual soul: to free- 23-25
dom from death-rebirth, or to bondage. The former is
allegorically the 'Northern' path, which here indicates
the way of light and brightness of day, symbolically a
cloudless sky. This leads selfless souls (those who are
free of ignorance and egoism) to the supreme Godhead. The other is the 'Southern' path, here meaning
the way of darkness or the path of smoke or fog. This
leads selfish souls (the ignorant, egoistic ones) to the
lesser light of the moon and chains them to the darkness of rebirth and death.

"These two ways, the light (Northern) and the dark 26
(Southern), have existed since the beginning. Following the light way (which refers not to a period of time
but a state of mind) leads you to spiritual success and
freedom; taking the dark way leads you to further
pain and misery.

"Once you know these two paths you can never be 27
deluded or misled again. Therefore, beloved friend,
gain this great knowledge! Be a *yogi* at all times.

"The wise know that living by scriptural injunctions 28
(good deeds, sacrifice, and so forth) will help you

reach heaven. But the true *yogi* knows that even heaven is part of nature (*prakriti*) and thus is eventually perishable. This *yogi* therefore transcends all of nature to reach Me, Brahman, the Imperishable Godhead, the Divine Love who lives in your heart."

CHAPTER 9

ROYAL KNOWLEDGE
AND THE KING OF SECRETS
(*Rajavidya Rajaguhya Yoga*)

*"I accept with joy whatever I am offered in true devotion:
fruit or water, leaf or flower. The gift is love,
the dedication of your heart."*

"Since you are so receptive, Arjuna, I will now reveal the most mysterious and profound secret. Having this knowledge will liberate you from the sorrows of worldly existence. This is the royal road of ultimate knowledge, the king of secrets — knowledge of both the visible and invisible Godhead. This is purifying knowledge, fully in accord with *dharma* (truth-based living). It is easy to practice and a joy to hold. Once you know this secret you cannot lose it.

1–2

"But those who lack faith in this doctrine will fail to find Me. To cynical people with trifling objections this secret is a closed book; they are compelled to return to the cycle of death and rebirth."

3

The Divine Mystery Unveiled

4-6 "I, Brahman, the Supreme Godhead, in My unmanifested (invisible) form, pervade everything and every creature in the universe. I am the origin of everything that is and is not. All beings in all the worlds exist, in spirit, within Me and depend on Me. But I do not abide in them because that would limit Me. This is the Divine mystery of Me as the unmanifested Godhead. I am never confined, attached, changed, or in any way limited. As birds fly across the sky leaving no trace, I, like the sky, am ever Myself, unaffected by anything of the phenomenal world.

7 "At the end of a *kalpa,* a cosmic day of Brahma (consisting of a full cycle of earthly eons, billions of years), all beings dissolve into My unmanifested matter, which at that point is the seed of their next coming to be. Then, at the beginning of the next cycle I generate them again, sending them onward at the moment of creation.

8 "Again and again I animate nature to bring forth this multitude of forms and beings, infusing spirit into their matter and subjecting all to the laws of their own nature.

9 "None of these actions in any way binds Me, Arjuna. I remain unattached and unconcerned, indifferent to the fruits of these actions. Nature, because of its proximity to Divinity, carries on the activities of creation.

10 "Under My watchful eye the laws of nature take their course. With Me presiding over the proceedings, the animate and inanimate manifest and the wheel of the world is set revolving.

"People who are unaware of My transcendent majesty   11
cannot relate to Me. They do not know that I am their
very soul. They disregard Me when I come to the
world clad in a body and relate to Me as just an ordinary mortal.

"Their ignorance makes their lives fraught with pain   12
and disaster. The selfish ones, their minds ever agitated and never in peace, lead a hurtful life. The sloth-
ful ones live a lazy life of ignorance, seeking only to
satisfy their bodily needs. All hopes and actions of
these ignorant souls are in vain.

"But the great souls (*mahatmas*) are different. Guided   13–14
by their more Divine nature and knowing My true
nature, they love Me and offer constant devotion to
Me — and they bear great love for all others.

"As the mind takes on the coloring of that which it
constantly glorifies, these people, steadfastly revering
Me and always absorbed in Me (God), literally *become*
this love. They turn godlike and eventually merge
in Me.

"Other great souls, those on the path of knowledge,   15
venerate Me as the one God in the many. They have
come to know that My attributes and forms are inex-
haustible. They see My million faces in everyone and
everything. To them all things and all beings in the
universe are aspects of this one Self, God.

"Because I am endless, the variety of ways I am adored   16
is endless. I am the rites and rituals of the scriptures. I
am the offerings made to the ancestors. I am the food
that is medicinal and nourishing. I am the formative

thought behind the chanted hymn (*mantra*). I am the gift offered into the fire; I am even the flame itself that consumes the offering.

"Apart from Me, Arjuna, there is absolutely no thought, no object, and no act. Holding this huge idea constantly in your awareness is indeed the way to reach Me.

17   "I am the father, mother, and grandfather of this universe. I am the one who dispenses the fruits of people's actions, their *karma*. I am the one thing worth knowing, and I am the enabler of all knowing. As water gets purified by filtering through earth, and other things get purified by being washed in water, mankind gets purified by contact with Me. I am the syllable *Om,* the very sound of Divinity. I am all the scriptures ever written.

18   "I am the goal at the end of all paths. I am the landlord of all creation. I am the inner witness in every human. I am your only lasting shelter; all beings dwell in Me. I am your best friend who lives in your heart as your conscience. I am the beginning of creation, the well-wisher of it, and the dissolution of it. I am the storehouse into which all life returns when creation dissolves — and I am the everlasting, imperishable seed from which it again springs.

19   "I give the heat of the sun. I let loose the food-giving rain, and I withhold it. I am both immortality and death (doled out based on the fruits of one's actions). I am both being and nonbeing. In My visible form I am the cosmos; in My invisible form I am the germ that lies hidden."

Humanity Gets What It Seeks

"Those who follow rituals and refrain from bad deeds, who offer worship and pray for heaven — they eventually reach those heavenly planes and share in celestial pleasures. But when the merits they earned in life are spent, they return to this world for yet another birth-death cycle. Caught by their own attachment to enjoyment, even the joy of heaven, they continue to come and go.   20–21

"Now listen carefully, Arjuna, this is the king of secrets, the crown jewel, the law of life at the spiritual level. If you think of Me only and constantly revere and worship Me with your mind and heart undistracted, I will personally carry the burden of your welfare; I will provide for your needs and safeguard what has already been provided.   22

"Just as the baby in the womb gets protection and nourishment due to its connection with the mother, humans also get refuge when connected with Me. But this is even greater than the baby-mother relationship because this shelter is for eternity!

"Those who faithfully make offerings to other deities are really worshiping Me, though by a more limited path. I, the Divinity in all, am the receiver and enjoyer of all offerings, all worship, all devotion. Minor gods give those who pray to them things of the world that only entangle them more in the earthly. I alone have the power to fulfill people's prayers without snarling them in attachments. I do this to increase their devotion and further their spiritual development.   23–24

25   "Those who worship minor gods go to the gods they
      pray to. Those who worship their ancestors (*manes*)
      are reunited with them after death. Those who wor-
      ship elemental spirits (*bhutas*) become like them. All
      these only add to earthly attachments. But those who
      worship Me come to Me, the Supreme Reality.

26   "I accept with joy whatever I am offered in true devo-
      tion: fruit or water, leaf or flower. The gift is love, the
      dedication of your heart. Devotion alone gains access
      to Divinity.

27   "Therefore, Arjuna, whatever you do in the world,
      whatever you eat, sacrifice, give up, or give away —
      even your suffering — offer it all to Me. Dedicate
      everything to Me, Divinity.

28   "By offering all your actions to the Divine you sur-
      render selfish attachment to their fruits, and this frees
      you from the *karmic* consequences of your actions —
      whether the consequences are pleasant or painful.
      With your mind unshakably on this path of renunci-
      ation you will be united with Me.

29   "I am equally present in all beings and show the same
      face to all creation; none are favored, none are hate-
      ful, and none dear. But those who love Me with brim-
      ming heart become absorbed in Me, and as they dwell
      in Me, I am revealed dwelling within them.

30-31 "I dwell even in the misguided. Know, Arjuna, that
      the change from profligacy to purity is not uncom-
      mon. If a person soiled with the wayward actions of a
      lifetime but turns to Me in utter devotion, I see no
      sinner. Newfound dedication can quickly refashion
      one's nature. Know this for certain: no one devoted to
      Me falls!

"Everyone who takes refuge in Me, whatever their   32
birth, gender, or position in society will attain the
supreme goal of merging into Me. This is true even
for those whom society may scorn or consider to be
ineligible (women in some cultures, for example, or
lower classes in others). There is no such thing as a
sinful or wicked birth. Where there is a hurricane of
love in the mind and heart *all* human distinctions
vanish.

"You have found yourself born into this transient and   33–34
joyless world, Arjuna, so turn from it and take delight
in Me. Give all your love to Me. Adore Me, the One
Divine. Make all your acts an offering. Surrender to
Me. Make Divinity your fondest ideal and highest
goal. Set your heart and mind on Me as I here pre-
scribe, and you will indeed enter into My very being."

CHAPTER 10

THE DIVINE GLORIES
(*Vibhuti Yoga*)

*"I am the silence of things secret,
the wisdom of the wise."*

Krishna speaks: "I notice, O Warrior, that your heart 1
delights in My words of wisdom, so I will elaborate.

"Neither the gods nor the great sages really know My 2
beginning. As I am the origin of them all, My glory
remains only partially known to them. Like children
who repeatedly ask about their parents' birth and childhood, they can never fully understand, no matter how
much they inquire.

"Some wise ones intuit from glimpses and partial 3
knowledge that I, the Supreme Godhead, am the source

of all creation. Thus enlightened, they eagerly join their lives to Me and are freed from misdeeds.

4-5   "Certain godly attributes of ordinary humans are My creation. I am in all living beings as the following qualities: intellect, patience, wisdom (knowing *Atma*), peace of mind, self-restraint, control of ego, discrimination (distinguishing Real from not-Real), equanimity, nonharm to others, austerity (purification), self-discipline (*tapas*), charitable giving, and other positive traits. All these human refinements proceed from Divinity; all are aspects of God expressed in diverse ways.

6   "From My mind were born the seven great sages of antiquity, the four elders, and the fourteen officials (*manus*). The sages symbolize planes of consciousness; the elders stand for humanity's progenitors; the *manus* are symbolic of the group of administrators empowered to operate the universe. Everything issues from Me."

Knowing God's Glories, You Love Him

7   "Knowing these mystical details, you glimpse My Divine power. You know that whatever you sense or perceive in the entire cosmos is that power, and you therefore know that you could no more be separate from Me than you could be separate from your very life.

8   "Wise *yogis* love Me ceaselessly. They know that the love they are experiencing for Me is Me, for I *am* Love, Arjuna. Just as the good farmer puts all his attention on to the soil, concentrating his mind fully on cultivating the land, *yogis* give their minds and hearts fully to the Divine, knowing that God alone is the source of everything.

"With their attention and life vitality flowing to Me,   9
absorbed in Me, these *yogis* take delight in speaking of
Me with others of like mind. Nothing is dearer to
anyone than their life, Arjuna, and I *am* life! Devoting
one's life to Me brings boundless contentment.

"To those who give Me their whole hearts I confer   10-11
buddhi (beyond worldly intellect), the power of dis-
criminating between the Real and not-Real. As famil-
iarity with My power and glory grows they are ever
more ardently drawn to Me. I *am* their wisdom, Arjuna.
Out of compassion I choose to dwell in their hearts,
and from there I dispel dark ignorance with the light
of knowing that they are the Divinity within."

Arjuna, in awe, begins to review his dawning under-   12-15
standing of God's power and glories. "Dearest Krishna!
You *are* the Godhead, the Supreme Presence! In Your
manifested (visible) form You are the entire universe;
in Your unmanifested (invisible) form You exist as the
Godhead, Pure Consciousness.

"You are the underlying essence of all things, the origin and the dwelling place of everything visible and
invisible in this universe. You are all of nature, and yet
You are beyond that, everlasting. You are everywhere
in everything as the Omnipresent. Those who have
used special intuitive powers to understand and reach
You, extol this.

"Now from Your own lips You are confirming it! Ah,
and yet Your coming in this human body remains
unknown to even the gods! You alone know Your
glory in its entirety.

"Krishna, please tell me more about Your Divine glo-   16-18
ries. Tell me how I can develop constant awareness of

You. Tell me again, O Divine One, of Your powers and attributes, for I never grow weary of hearing of them."

19 Krishna replies, "Very well O warrior friend. Absorption in the attributes of the Divine is as good as absorption in Divinity itself. But because *all* the splendors of nature are attributes of My majesty, I will only give you a glimpse of a few. From this partial knowledge you may infer My infinitude.

20 "I am the innermost True Self, the *Atma* seated in the hearts of all beings. And I am the beginning, middle, and end of all beings.

21 "Of the deities presiding over light, I am the one for January, loved by all for turning the world's course toward warmth. Of the wind gods who bring immense good in the world, I am the whirlwind. Of the daytime luminaries I am the radiant sun, and of the lights of the night I am the moon.

22 "Of the ancient scriptures I am the foremost, the *Sama Veda.** Of the secondary gods I am Indra, the chief among them. Of the sense organs I am the mind that records all sensations. Of the numerous levels of life awareness that exist in all life-forms, I am Pure Consciousness.

23 "Of the eleven deities of destruction I am Shiva, destroyer of evil in the mind, who brings humanity's lasting welfare. And I am Rudra, who brings grace to humanity through sorrow. Of the celestial beings who

---

* *Sama* is the essence of other *vedas* set to music. The *vedas* comprise a mass of Divine knowledge in the form of scores of thousands of mystical and spiritual chants and aphorisms.

acquire and hoard wealth (*Yakshas* and *Rakshasas*), I am their king, Kubera, the lord of fabulous wealth. Of the eight elements in the structure of nature (earth, fire, water, air, space, mind, intellect, and ego), I am fire, the one who brings warmth and life. And of all mountains I am Mount Meru, which in the human structure equates with the life force in the spinal column.

"Of the high spiritual teachers who administer the code of conduct, know Me to be Brihaspati, the Chief Priest, Holy even among the gods. Among the warrior-chiefs I am Skanda, who leads the world to victory over the demons. Of all the bodies of water I am the ocean, into which all the rest merge. 24

"Among the *rishis* (seers) I am Bhrigu, ever in the highest plane of superconsciousness. Of sacrifices I am the most potent, *japa*, repetition of the name of the Divine. Of all utterances I am *Om*, the most sacred of sound symbols. And of fixed, stationary things I am the Himalayas. 25

"Of the trees, Arjuna, I am the holy fig tree (*Ashvatta*, the *peepul* tree), which represents the 'upside-down' tree of life with its roots above in spirit and its branches below in the earth. Among the most spiritually enlightened Divinities I am Narada, the foremost of those who teach the principle of unity amidst the world's vast diversity. Of the celestial beings I am their king, Chitraratha. Of those high-perfected souls (*siddhas*) I am Kapila, the best of the best. 26

"Of horses I am *Ucchiasravas*, the nectar-born one. Of elephants I am *Airavata*, the one from the sea of milk. And of all humans, I am born as royalty, the monarch. 27

28   "Of weapons I am God's thunderbolt, which descends on wickedness. Of cows I am *Kamadhenu,* the celestial milk cow of cheerful and willing mind with the power to satisfy all requirements of life. Among instincts I am the procreative urge. Of snakes I am *Vasuki,* god of snakes, symbol of *kundalini,* the coiled up reservoir of cosmic energy in each person.

29   "Among nonpoisonous snakes I am *Ananta,* symbol of the five elements of nature, on whom I rest. Of water deities I am *Varuna,* their king. I am the presiding deity of the departed ancestors (*Aryama*). And of the controllers of the universe I am *Yama,* the god of death.

30   "Of those who defy evil, iniquity, and injustice, I am *Prahlada,* who is virtuous even though he is the son of the sworn enemy of the gods. Among those who keep records I am the unfailing reckoner, Time itself. Of animals I am the lion. Of birds I am the Lord's eagle, *Garuda.*

31   "Of the four purifiers in nature — earth, water, fire, and air — I am the wind, which purifies the other purifiers. Of those who wield deadly weapons I am *Rama,* who uses his weapon only for the good of humanity. Of all fish I am the shark, the most powerful. Among rivers I am Ganges with its sanctifying water.

32   "Of all things created, Arjuna, I am the beginning, the middle, and end. Of all sciences I am spiritual knowledge — *Atma* knowledge — the science of Self that makes ignorance vanish. Of all humanity's instruments for inquiry and debate, I am pure logic.

33   "Of the sum total of all sound in the cosmos I am the letter A. In grammar I am the compound word, the

most powerful of words. As I am time itself, I am without beginning and end. I mete out the *karma* of all beings, and thus am called the Disburser-Whose-Face-Is-Turned-Everywhere.

"I am the certain death that devours all, and I am also 34 the seed of all that are to be. Of the qualities that, due to their grace and tenderness, are termed 'female,' I am fame and fortune, sweet speech, memory, intelligence, steadfast perseverance, loyalty, and forgiveness.

"Of the great *Sama Vedas* I am the best (*Brihat* 35 *Saman*). Of poetic meters I am the foremost, the *Gayatri* adoration. Of the months, I am *Margasirsha* (parts of November-December), the most favorable time for spiritual practice. Of the seasons, I am the flowery spring.

"Among deceitful practices I am the roll of the dice. I 36 am the splendor and radiance of the physically strong. Of that which takes humanity forward, I am effort. Of the three constituents of nature I am goodness (*sattva*).

"Among the Vrishni clan I am Krishna. Among the 37 Pandavas I am Arjuna. Among the great, God-realized sages I am Vyasa, known as an incarnation of Divinity. Among the omniscient seers (*kavis*) I am Usana, the foremost of them.

"Among those who punish others I am the scepter, the 38 symbol of measured justice. I am the art of statesmanship in those who seek victory by noble means. I am the silence of things secret. I am the wisdom of the wise.

"O Arjuna, beloved comrade, I am the source of 39 everything in creation, the origin of all beings, all lives. In fact, I am whatever can be thought, imagined, or conceived. Nothing in this world, animate or inanimate, can exist without Me.

40–41   "There is no end to My Divine manifestations (*vibhutis*). What I have described is but a tiny glimpse into My glories. Whatever is beautiful, mighty, or glorious in this world has emanated from just a part of My infinite power.

42   "And finally, Arjuna, as this variety of details is of little use to you, just know that I, Brahman, exist, and that I stand holding this entire creation by a small fraction of My Supreme Glory."

CHAPTER 11

THE COSMIC VISION
(*Visvarupa Darsana Yoga*)

"Everywhere I look, there You are."

Arjuna sighs, his eyes glistening. "Thank You, Krishna, 1–2
for this wondrous revelation of Your glories; it has
removed my delusion. Thank You for Your detailed
account of the evolution and dissolution of beings, and
for Your exquisite description of Your splendor.

"I now know that You are what You say You are, Divine 3–4
One, but I would like to actually see You in Your true
God form, rather than just this Krishna body. If appro-
priate, and if I am worthy, please show me now."

Krishna says, "You are worthy, Arjuna. I will have you 5–7
behold millions of My shapes, forms, and colors, for

99

naught exists outside Me. And I will have you see within Me the many classes of celestial beings and more marvels not previously revealed. And you will view the entire creation of animate and inanimate beings concentrated within the Cosmic Me, and witness whatever else your inner thoughts may bring."

A Thousand Suns:
Krishna Reveals His Wondrous Cosmic Form

8   "But you cannot perceive any of this with human eyes composed of natural elements and thus able to grasp only physical nature. I will have to grant you special eyes to see beyond that. So now, using Divine vision, behold My Divine Cosmic Form."

9–11   Back in the chambers of the old blind king, Sanjaya begins describing the unfolding, his eyes wide in amazement. "O King!" Sanjaya exclaims, "Lord Krishna is all at once a marvelous sight: thousands of facial features, countless mouths and eyes, clothes adorned with ornaments of beauty never seen before. He's holding many weapons uplifted as symbols of His infinite powers, showing Himself arrayed in heavenly garments, garlands of flowers — I can even smell His celestial perfumes. He seems to be facing in all directions!

12   "It is impossible to describe in earthly words the dazzling light emanating from Him — it is as if a thousand suns were suddenly blazing in the sky; even that is insufficient tribute to the splendor and brilliance of His aura.

13   "Arjuna is now 'seeing' the entire universe, with all its myriad forms, within Krishna's cosmic body — planets, distant stars, living beings, multitudes of animals,

the vast plant kingdom — all expressions of the same consciousness that lives within the Divine One. The celestial worlds are also there for Arjuna to see; all the regions within and without are all united, concentrated at once within this vision of the Supreme One; all contained within the one being, the Divinity of Divinities."

Arjuna gasps, "It's awesome, Krishna! I bow my head in reverence to You. I can hardly find my voice. I . . . I see things I've never seen or heard about or even conceived. I see all the deities, O Divine One, and all kinds of living creatures within Your being. I see all the multitudes of lesser deities and animals that You earlier proclaimed to exist. I see all the seers and saints, and celestial serpents — all these beings are contained in You! 14–15

"But I cannot see to the far reaches of You, Krishna. I see no limits to Your Cosmic God form, no boundaries or demarcation points to Your spectrum of existence. I see countless eyes and arms, mouths, and bellies, but I find no end or beginning to it all. It simply is, without any restrictions of space or time or thought. 16–17

"I perceive crowns, and all the tools and symbols of Your rule over the worlds. The luminosity surrounding You is so brilliant it's hard on even these Divine eyes that You granted me.

"From all this I can only conclude that You are indeed the Imperishable Supreme Being, the one and only thing to be known. You are the ultimate refuge for all, the guardian and support for the universe. You are the very basis of the universe's functioning, what is called the Eternal *Dharma*. You are the everlasting Cosmic 18

Spirit (*Purusha*). I am now convinced of these truths, O beloved Krishna.

19 "And I see You as birthless and deathless with total, absolute power and strength, as if possessing a million arms. Your mouth is the fire that warms the universe, and Your radiance lights it as though the sun and moon were Your eyes.

20 "Your vast, limitless presence fills all the space between heaven and earth, and extends far beyond all that. You *are* all-pervasive! I also see fierceness and terror in You, Krishna, and I watch beings in all the three worlds* tremble.

21–22 "Hordes of deities swirl around You and enter into Your being. Some are awestruck and fearfully extol Your praises. Legions of other celestial beings sing rapturous hymns in praise of Your awesome purifying powers. Even these high beings gaze at Your fiery eyes in amazement, unable to gauge Your universal figure in its entirety."

Krishna Reveals the Battle's Cosmic Inevitability

23–25 "O Krishna, it's breathtaking. No matter how far I turn in any direction, high or low, side to side, I cannot see an end to Your form. All I see is Your vastness brushing the sky and horizons; I lose my sense of direction and feel utterly lost and bewildered. And now, seeing Your measureless might, it's as though millions of arms and teeth are set to devour everything in sight.

---

* Referring to Earth, in-between planes, the heavens; and the three states of consciousness: the waking, dream, and deep sleep states.

"I perceive all the worlds and creatures become as I feel inside, frightened and terror-struck at Your fury. When I crane my neck to look upon Your gaping mouths and grinding teeth I am filled with horror; my peace of mind flees from me. Be gracious, O Krishna, please show mercy!

"I watch all the enemy forces — the sons of the old blind king, generals, heroes, relatives, others who allied themselves with them — all are rushing head-long into Your immensity as though being devoured. And I watch as vast numbers of our own soldiers and warrior-chiefs also rush heedless into the maw. I hear the frightful cries as these forces are ground up and crushed within You. Like flooded rivers rushing toward the ocean, the heroes on both sides are scurrying, stumbling to their awful fate in You; like moths flitting purposely into the flame, they rush to their doom in You. It is as though You are swallowing up the worlds and licking Your lips, O Lord. Your destructiveness is as a fierce blaze filling the sky, permeating the universe! *26–30*

"When You are so ruinous and fierce, the reality of You abruptly hides from me. I suddenly don't know who You are or what Your purpose is. Who are You? Help me find my balance!" *31*

Krishna answers, "I *am* Time, Arjuna — and now, here at this place of battle, I am the mighty world-destroying Time. With or without you, the warriors are arrayed to fight, and whether on the righteous or corrupt side, they are readied for their ruin and must die. The destruction of enemies is inevitable. It is not possible for an individual person to avert the design of Divinity. *32*

33   "Therefore, attack, O mighty warrior, conquer your evil-doing enemies and win kingdom, wealth, and fame. I have willed to wipe out wickedness and have therefore already slain these warriors. Your actions will only be My outward cause, and you are merely My instrument.

34   "Although they are indeed brave, nevertheless smite them, for they are already doomed. Fight and you will win. Killing them is not contrary to *dharma* (righteousness)."

35   Arjuna interrupts, "I am shaking in fear, Divine One," he says. "I bow my head and join my palms to You. My voice is so choked and my lips so trembling I can hardly speak.

36–37   "It is indeed appropriate, O Divinity, that the world reveres You, that the celestials bow to You and the demons flee from You. How could they not be in awe of You? You are the Cause of the Cause, the Eternal that existed even before Brahma the Creator. You transcend time itself, space itself, and even causation! You are the Supreme Divinity of all deities, the Lord of all gods. You are That within which the universe dwells. You are the Everlasting. You are That which is and That which is not, and even beyond both That and Not-That; You are rightly called the Supreme Absolute Reality.

38   "What else can rapturous souls do but extol You, the first and highest among gods, the most ancient spirit? Within You the cosmos rests in safety, and into You it will dissolve. You are at once the Knower and known, both the Goal and our striving toward it. Indeed, Your form fills and overflows the universe."

Arjuna, Overwhelmed, Seeks Forgiveness

"You are the wind itself, Krishna, not merely the lord   39–40
of it. You are death itself, fire, water, and the moon
itself, not merely the lord over them. You are the
father of all born, and the sire of the fathers. Please
accept my upwelling of devotion to You. I salute You
a thousand times. Take these salutes, Divine One,
from every quarter of Your creation. Infinite and
measureless is Your might, and boundless is Your
glory! Everywhere I look, there You are. Indeed, You
are all there is.

"I haven't really comprehended Your greatness until   41–42
now, O Divine One. In the past I carelessly called You
by Your familiar names and took You to be merely a
fellow mortal, calling You simply 'friend.' If I have
shown disrespect while we played as children or while
resting or eating or in the company of others, please
forgive me. I hereby take on a most reverent attitude.

"Who can match Your might? You are the source of all   43
things in this world, animate or inanimate. You are the
adored Master. None in all three worlds is equal to You.

"I prostrate myself before You and ask You to forgive   44
me! As a friend forgives a comrade or a father forgives
a son, or a mother forgives a child, or a lover forgives
a beloved — please grant me pardon, Divine One.

"I am delighted to have been shown this rare vision,   45–46
but I'm still filled with fear by it. Please have mercy on
me, show me You as You were before. Let me see the
familiar shape I knew — not with a thousand arms
but with two — or even the four arms You occasionally seemed to have due to Your great strength."

Only Through My Grace and Your Love

47–48   Krishna responds: "Through My Divine power and grace you have received this vision of My cosmic form. No other has seen this but you. I showed you this because I love you, Arjuna. This vision cannot be won through spiritual practices, study, service, rituals, or severe penance. Only through My grace has this sight of Me come, and it has come only to you.

49   "So why fear, Arjuna? Look, here I am as I appeared before. Be alarmed no more. Be happy, take courage."

50–51   Lord Krishna reverts to His human form, a slight smile on His lips. Arjuna says, "O Krishna, I am very happy to see You back, and I'm beginning to feel calmer, like my old self."

52   Krishna says, "The cosmic form you saw is extremely rare. Even celestial beings — those who are more spiritually elevated than humans but with no higher knowledge of the Godhead — even they yearn to see My form.

53   "Neither by study of the scriptures nor by personal austerities for purification, neither by giving gifts to the deserving nor by performing rituals nor by making offerings to Me can anyone behold Me as you have, Arjuna. Those spiritual activities — studying, gift giving, rituals, and so forth — are conducive to purifying the mind, but they will not bring the vision of Me.

54   "And yet, through unswerving, single-minded love (*ananya bhakti*), humans *can* know the essence of My supreme glory and can enter into My Being. How? Pure devotion, Arjuna. In a constant state of deep

love for God, a true devotee recognizes nothing but God.

"So therefore, O Prince, dedicate all your actions to 55 Me. Work for Me alone with no attachments or self-ish desires. Make Me your exclusive goal. Take refuge in Me. Love Me wholeheartedly and bear no malice toward any creature. Then you will reach Me."

CHAPTER 12

THE PATH OF LOVE
(*Bhakti Yoga*)

"I love the one who is beyond 'I' and 'mine,'
unperturbed by pain and not elated by pleasure."

Arjuna speaks again: "My interest is aroused now but I ₁
have a question. You say that only by unswerving love
and worship can a devotee attain oneness with God.
But some worship the invisible, formless God (*Nirguna*
Brahman) and others worship the visible God with
form (*Saguna* Brahman). Which of these two aspects is
easiest? Which will melt your heart more?"

Krishna answers, "I am pleased with either path, but ₂
worshiping *Saguna* Brahman, the one you can see, is
right for you at this point, Arjuna. Setting your heart
steadily on the visible aspect of Me and becoming saturated with devotion and faith will lead you quickly and
surely to Me, the Godhead.

3–4   "As for those who worship *Nirguna* Brahman (God without form or name), if they truly subdue their senses, maintain a calm mind, and work for the good of all beings, they also come to Me. But realize, Arjuna, that *Nirguna* means not of nature; this Brahman is indefinable and unmanifested, invisible, not materialized. The senses therefore have no access to it, there is nothing to which it can be likened.

5   "Devotees of the nonmaterialized Godhead have a steeper climb. It is extremely difficult for a person in a physical form to really understand the formless. Ordinary people identify themselves with their own physical body and cannot help but conceptualize God as also being in some sort of body. To deeply love the formless God one must be free from one's own body consciousness, and this state is not attainable by many.

"But keep in mind, Arjuna, that worshiping Divinity in a form will help for only a while. Those whose ultimate aim is full liberation must sooner or later give up attachment to the body. Without this, the *Atma* stage of spiritual development cannot be attained."

The Order of Devotion

6–7   "But know, Arjuna, that I quickly come to those who offer Me all their actions, set their minds on Me with unswerving devotion, worship Me as their dearest delight, and take Me as their one and only goal in life. Because they so dearly love Me, I save them from the sorrow of death and endless waves of rebirth.

8   "It is true that one is where one's mind is. So fix your mind on Me. Be absorbed in Me alone. Focus your devotion on Me. Still yourself in Me. Without a doubt you will then come and live within Me.

"If you are unable to become absorbed in Me, wean   9
your mind away from the world and reach Me by constantly concentrating on Me. I know this may seem
impossible, but as I said, the 'impossible' can be made
possible through regular practice (*abhyasa yoga*).

"If you find that you are not disciplined enough to con-   10
centrate in this manner, transform all your worldly
actions into worship. Do them for My sake. Turn your
force of habit to your own advantage; make a habit of
dedicating all your actions to Divinity. In this way you
become My instrument and your mind gradually
becomes purified, which will lead you to Me.

"But if you cannot even do that, then pursue an alter-   11
native that is equally powerful. Take refuge in Me.
Subdue your mind and give up desire for the fruits of
your actions.

"Knowledge is better than mere performance of ritu-   12
als. Meditation is better than knowledge. Abandoning
the fruits of one's acts (*tyaga*), is better than meditation. Why? Because peace *immediately* follows the giving up of expectations."

The Most Loved Devotees

"Arjuna, I will now enumerate the marks of the devo-   13–14
tee I most dearly love. I love the one who harbors no
ill will toward any living being, who returns love for
hatred, who is friendly and compassionate toward all.
I love the devotee who is beyond 'I' and 'mine,'
unperturbed by pain and not elated by pleasure, who
possesses firm faith, is forgiving, ever contented and
ever meditating on Me.

"I love the peaceful devotee who is neither a source of   15
agitation in the world nor agitated by the world. I love

those who are free of fear, envy, and other annoyances that the world brings, who accept the knocks that come their way as blessings in disguise.

16   "I love those who do their worldly duties uncon-cerned and untroubled by life. I love those who expect absolutely nothing. Those who are pure both internally and externally are also very dear to Me. I love the devotees who are ready to be My instrument, meet any demands I make on them, and yet ask noth-ing of Me.

17   "I love those who do not rejoice or feel revulsion, who do not grieve, do not yearn for possessions, are not affected by the bad or good things that happen to and around them and yet are full of devotion to Me. They are dear to Me because they live in the Self (*Atma*), not in the commotion of the world.

18–19 "I love devotees whose attitudes are the same toward friend or foe, who are indifferent to honor or ignominy, heat or cold, praise or criticism — who not only control their talking but are silent within. Also very dear to Me are those generally content with life and unattached to things of the world, even to home. I love those whose sole concern in life is to love Me. Indeed, these and all the others I mentioned are very, very dear to Me.

20   "Hold Me as your highest goal. Live your life in accordance with the immortal wisdom I have taught you here, and practice this wisdom with great faith and deep devotion. Surrender your mind and heart completely to Me. Then I will love you dearly, and you will go beyond death to immortality."

Part 3

ATTAINING
LIBERATION
NOW

CHAPTER 13

THE FIELD AND ITS KNOWER: DISTINGUISHING BETWEEN MATTER AND SPIRIT
(*Kshetra Kshetrajna Vibhaga Yoga*)

"When the body falls...
it is the spirit that remains standing."

Arjuna asks, "If Divinity is everything in the world, Krishna, then what is the difference between the world and Divinity? How can one distinguish between one's worldly body and godly soul? What is the difference between physical matter and the world of Spirit? And is there any benefit in learning this?"

Krishna responds, "These are important questions, Arjuna. When you know the true nature of the material world your grief is destroyed; when you understand the true nature of the Spirit, bliss is acquired.

"The term *field* denotes one's physical body and everything else in the material world. The *Knower of the Field* signifies the intelligent principle that resides in, but is not really a part of, the body and all matter. This indwelling intelligence is the mysterious entity within that is close enough to watch what goes on in the 'field' and yet stands somewhat separate from it. It is also referred to as soul, or *Atma*.

2   "Arjuna, I am the Knower of the Field, the Indweller in everybody and everything. I am the innermost Self, the soul, the *Atma* in all beings. The ability to discriminate between the field and its Knower is the utmost highest knowledge, as it requires a true understanding of both secular things and sacred knowing. So listen carefully."

The Field (Prakriti, *the World of Nature*)

3   "I will now further explain what the field — the world of nature — consists of, where it came from, and why and how it operates. Then I will tell you more of the Knower of the Field and the powers of the Knower.

4   "Though quite intricate, this is a wondrous inquiry, Arjuna. The great sages in prehistoric times discovered these profound truths through meditation and precise reasoning. Down through the ages they expressed them through chants and aphorisms (*vedas*), carefully balancing their deep love for God with rigorous questioning and understanding so that these truths would appeal jointly to the heart and the head.

5-6   "First, understand that truly knowing the field, the natural world (*prakriti*), is not simply a process of listing the myriad items that comprise it. To understand nature itself it is necessary to know something about human consciousness. To *know* something is to be conscious of it. You become conscious of things in the world (that is, you 'know' them) through the mechanisms of perception in your nervous system — sight, hearing, feeling, mind, and so forth. But the nervous system is itself a part of nature; that which you use to know the world, nature, is also nature. Thus, that which is known cannot really be separated from the knower of it.

"Also understand, Arjuna, that *all* of the natural world, all of *prakriti,* originates in consciousness itself — the One Supreme Consciousness, Divinity. In the natural world Supreme Consciousness separates into many forces both physical and mental — endlessly combining and recombining. Everything known or knowable stems from Consciousness. Knowing this, one really knows the field.

"The following are the twenty-five components of nature, the field:

"First, there is the 'unmanifested' (the *mahat,* literally 'the great cause'). This is a latent reasoning force, the first glimmering of an ego sense in the cosmos, an early, raw capacity to differentiate and decide — like a seed that drinks in moisture and is about to swell in size prior to sprouting. It is this 'unmanifested' that gives rise to mind, matter, and energy.

"From this first comes the higher mind (intellect, *buddhi*), the discriminatory faculty, the ability to distinguish between Real and not-Real (between the spiritual Self and worldly self).

"From *buddhi* comes the ego that we know, the principle of individuation (*ahamkara*), which causes one to be aware of one's self as an apparently separate entity.

"From the ego principle is produced the lower mind (*manas,* usually referred to simply as 'mind'). Its job is to receive through the senses and process the messages received from the field, and carry them to the intellect. Included here are certain subtle modifications of mind: desire and aversion, pleasure and pain, the experience of one's physical body, intelligence (the power to interpret), and the mental experience of physical stamina.

"Emerging from this level of mind are the ten sense organs (*indriyas*), which are not physical *organs* per se but powerful sensory mechanisms or capabilities. There are two sets: the five 'organs' of perception (hearing, touch, sight, taste, and smell), and the five organs of action (vocal cords, hands, feet, the reproductive and generative organs, and elimination organs).

"From these ten sense organs develop the five so-called 'objects of the senses,' which are not solid objects but the subtle essences in the world that attract the senses. These 'sense objects' are sound (audibility, resonance, sonority); feeling (tactility, texture, tangibility); aspect (the *look* of something — shape, color, brightness); taste (gustation, flavor, savoriness); and smell (olfaction, odors, scents, fragrances).

"Lastly produced are the five age-old categories of components into which the mind organizes all worldly matter — the five basic elements of earth, water, fire, air, and space.

"Those are the twenty-four constituents of inert matter that comprise the field. There is actually one more: the mysterious vital force, *Atma,* that infuses life into all this material. This makes up the total twenty-five."

The Knower of the Field
(Purusha, *Cosmic Consciousness)*

"Arjuna, I will now turn from the field to the qualities of the Knower of the Field. This intuitive knowledge is beyond intellectual knowing. It comes through possessing distinctive virtues and outlooks that, taken together, give rise to such knowing.   7

"The Knower of the Field is humble and harmless. Be like this Knower. Know in your heart that all excellence emanates only from the Divine. Be gentle. Be forgiving of any hurt received. Be upright and harmonized in thought, word, and deed. Serve your teacher and imbibe his or her good traits and disposition. Be steadfast in your spiritual development. Be pure of mind — escape the worldly deluge of mental pollution, because purity is indispensable to your spiritual growth. Be ever in control of your body, mind, and senses.

"Be detached from egoism, selfishness, and the attractions of the world. Do not see yourself as this body-mind complex that suffers the pains of bondage to birth, aging, death, and rebirth. Know instead that you are *Atma,* the Eternal Reality beyond all that.   8

"Meet the inevitable good and bad of life with an even mind. To no one or no thing be a slave! Be tied neither to possessions nor family. Love and fulfill your   9 responsibilities to spouse, children, home, and kin, but do not become so identified with them that you forget *Atma,* your True Self Within.

10   "The way to do all this is through loving Me with your heart undistracted. Be ever intent on Divinity. Center all your thoughts on Me. Turn your back on social life and the commotion of the crowds. Prefer for now the company of like-minded persons, and then, as you advance, sever even from them — but not as a hermit, as a detached *yogi.*

11   "Grow in wisdom through diligent inquiry into the nature of Self and non-Self. Only Divinity is Truth, Arjuna, and *Atma* is truly Divinity. This I declare to be true knowledge. To seek anything else is to seek ignorance."

Knowing the Knower

12   Krishna continues, "I will now tell you what you need to know to go beyond death to immortality. The goal of spiritual wisdom is to *realize* — to know in your heart — the Supreme Godhead that is both being and nonbeing, both manifested and unmanifested.

13–15   "The Godhead dwells in all creation, in all hands and feet, in the heads of all beings as their eyes, ears, and mouths. It is Itself devoid of senses, yet Its subtle powers perform the tasks of the senses. This Divinity is totally independent, yet It supports all things. The Godhead is beyond the three *gunas* of nature, yet It is the very consciousness in them. It is inside and outside all beings. It is both formless and with form. It moves and does not move. Its subtlety and mystery is incomprehensible to the nonpurified mind. To the

ignorant the Godhead is distant; to the knowledgeable It is very near.

"Divinity is subtle and beyond comprehension. It 16
appears to be many but is one undivided. Divinity
sends creation out from within Itself; It protects creation, preserves it, and dissolves it.

"As the Lighter of all lights, the Godhead, Brahman, 17
dwells in each and every heart, beyond the darkness of
ignorance. It is the True Self Within, the sole goal of
knowledge; and indeed It is Knowledge Itself.

"That is the truth about the field and its Knower 18
(about matter and Spirit, body and Soul). Devoted
people who grow to understand this profound, mysterious truth are worthy to be united with Me."

The Union of the Field and Its Knower

"Also know, Arjuna, that both nature and Spirit, both 19
prakriti (the field) and *Purusha* (Pure Consciousness),
are without beginning. Know that all of physical
nature evolves from Consciousness. And know that
all of nature and all the attributes in nature are nothing but the permutation and combination of the
three *guna*-qualities of nature I mentioned earlier:
calm goodness (*sattva*), passionate action (*rajas*), and
dark lethargy (*tamas*). And know that nature
(*prakriti*) alone is the source of everything in the
physical universe.

"The cause of your body is nature (*prakriti*), but the 20
cause of your aliveness — your experience of being an
individual, feeling joy and sorrow in a particular body
— is Spirit (*Purusha*).

21   "This Spirit-self (*jiva*) that takes residence in a material body forgets its true nature (*Atma*) and mistakenly identifies itself with that body. Thus it becomes attached to nature, to the *gunas.* While the individual is a mixture of all three *guna* qualities, the one to which it is most attached predominates, and the individual becomes that type of person, experiencing the behaviors, sensations, and delusions that are peculiar to that quality — becoming a generally calm (*sattvic*) person, an active (*rajasic*) person, or a lethargic (*tamasic*) person. As the individual is now a part of nature, it is bound to participate in repeated births and deaths, the painful destiny of all matter.

22   "And yet, remember, Arjuna, that the Spirit (*Purusha* energy) dwelling in the individual body as *Atma* is truly Brahman, the Godhead. This Supreme Being is spoken of as the following: the Observer who watches and referees the game of life, the Approver who permits it all to happen, the Supporter who helps it all to happen, the Enjoyer who experiences it all with gusto but knows it is a game, and most important, the Master who holds complete dominion over all the events though being unaffected by any of them.

23   "When you have directly experienced the Godhead (Brahman), you will not be born again because then you will truly know that the Divine One is beyond all this natural world of *prakriti* and *gunas.* The fire of this great knowledge will burn out all your *karmas,* and there will be no more motivating force within you to create another birth. Thus unburdened, you (in this state, called *jivanmukti*) will duly perform all your duties in the world and yet watch life in total peace.

24   "The paths to this great knowledge are several. Some realize it by building mind power through meditation

(*dhyana yoga*); others do it by sharpening the intellect through acquisition of knowledge (*jnana yoga*); and yet others through performing selfless action (*karma yoga*). Whichever the path, if successfully walked it eventually develops pure, single-minded love for God (*bhakti yoga,* union with God through devotion). When one reaches this level of absolute Divine Love one reaches the End.

"For those unable to grasp any of these paths there is another way. By diligently and faithfully listening to their spiritual teachers and worshiping the Divine as instructed, they too will eventually pass beyond the wheel of death and rebirth. 25

"Return for a moment, Arjuna, to consideration of the field. Remember that whatever comes into existence, whether thing or being, is a result of the union between matter and Spirit (the field and the Knower). 26

"When the matter part of this union falls in death, the spirit part remains standing. Ordinary people do not see the Spirit within and therefore think that it is their own self that dies. Only when you see the undying within the dying do you really see the Truth. 27

"Indeed, true seers, perceiving Divinity in everyone, do no harm to anyone. The ones who don't perceive this unity separate themselves from others, seeing some as friends and others as foes. These are the ones who do harm. It is this illusion of separateness that causes all evils perpetrated by humanity! How can one who really knows *Atma* injure the same *Atma* in another? As I have often repeated, the true seer of *Atma* reaches the Godhead and leaves death and rebirth behind. 28

29   "Seers of Truth are aware that all action is done by the body and not by the Spirit dwelling in the body (by *prakriti,* not *Purusha*). They know that the body belongs to nature, and *Atma* belongs to Spirit. Thus they understand that the True Self (*Atma*) is actionless, is never the doer.

30   "You must ultimately realize this tremendous lesson: All creatures, although appearing separate, are truly only one; all beings emanate from the Godhead and are united in the Godhead. The one who truly learns this *becomes* the Godhead and thereby attains liberation.

31   "The True Self (*Atma*), as I have said, has no beginning or end. It is beyond *prakriti.* Though dwelling in the field (the body), this Knower of the Field does not act. It is therefore untouched by the fruits of action and untainted by *karma,* good or bad.

32   "This True Self Within is indeed mysterious, Arjuna. It is subtler than the subtlest. As water, when it is steam (its subtle state), defies being dirtied by its surroundings, *Atma* is never tainted though it dwells in every creature.

33   "Just as the single sun illuminates the whole world, the sole Knower of the Field lights up the entire field. All beings great and small, saint and sinner, high and low, get their light — their consciousness — from this one source.

34   "Finally, Arjuna, know that the goal is not to get entangled in the world, but to use the world to reach Divinity. Use your eye of wisdom, your intuitive faculty, to distinguish between the field and the Knower. Then you can actually cut yourself free from the field, from bondage to the worldly, and reach Me, the Supreme Goal."

CHAPTER 14

GOING BEYOND THE THREE FORCES OF NATURE
(*Gunatraya Vibhaga Yoga*)

". . . beyond time, space, and circumstances to the place where the mind is tranquil and ego disappears."

"Arjuna, I will now explain in more detail the very nature of nature (*prakriti*), and how the three *gunas* function within each individual's life. The term *guna* refers not only to the three properties of nature but also to the corresponding three underlying attitudes of mind that shape all human behavior. When you know these secrets, you possess the spiritual wisdom that can take you beyond birth and death. Through this wisdom the sages were guided to supreme perfection. 1

"In fact, those who live by this wisdom definitely unite with Me and will not have to be reborn even when the cosmos is recreated at the dawn of a cycle. 2

3   "It is I who instills the seed of all births into the vast womb of nature (*prakriti*). Nature in turn gives birth to the infinitely diverse temperaments of all creatures.

4   "Everything that is born, Arjuna, comes from this subtle union of Spirit and nature. Whatever forms are produced in any of the wombs of the universe, know that My nature (*prakriti*) is the cosmic mother of all creation, and that I am the seed-giving father."

Gunas, *the Three Strands of Nature*

5   "All life evolves from the differentiating power of three forces or strands in nature: *sattva* (purity, light, calmness), *rajas* (passion, action), and *tamas* (ignorance, darkness, inertia).

"Everyone, Arjuna, has all three forces within them in differing proportions and will, as I have mentioned, exhibit the type of behavior that is in accord with their predominating *guna*. Thus, the *gunas* explain why you think, feel, speak, and act as you do. This is the entire map. The *sattvic* person (a rare type) will be calm and harmonized. *Rajasic* persons (certainly the majority) are full of restless energy. *Tamasic* people (also quite common) will be lethargic, indolent, and unmotivated to act.

"The word *guna* also means *strand* in a directly literal sense. *Gunas* are forces that weave together to form a strong rope that binds the Self (*Atma,* soul) to one's worldly body and thus to life, death, and rebirth.

"The objective of life is to reshape one's character upward in pursuit of a higher ideal — changing from indolence or inertia (*tamas*) into passionate effort (*rajas*), and then channeling that into calmness (*sattva*).

"Of these forces, *sattva,* being pure, provides an unob-   6
structed view of *Atma.* But even here a problem can
arise when one finds pleasure in sacred knowledge and
begins yearning for it. *Any* pleasure, even good pleasure, creates attachment and subsequent desire. All
attachments, even golden ropes, bind the individual
(*jiva*) to the pain and sadness of the material world.

"Desireful action is the very nature of *rajas,* the sec-   7
ond *guna.* Desire goads one into action and creates a
sense of doership in the mind. It spawns a thirst for
acquiring and clinging to worldly things — to people
and sensations that attract the senses. As fuel feeds
fire, *rajas* breeds attachments to action and its fruit.
This attachment turns on itself, bringing greed and
greed's close relative, anger.

"*Tamas* (literally *darkness*) is saturated with ignorance   8
and instills nothing but indolence and stupor. This
guna bewilders people, stealing their capacity for work
(their *rajasic* energy) as well as their composure (their
sattvic calmness).

"So, Arjuna, *sattva* ties the calm person to joy, *rajas*   9–10
binds active doers to incessant activity, and *tamas* fas-
tens indolent people to delusion and sloth. Over the
course of a day all three *gunas* ebb and flow within
each person. *Sattva* rises to the fore by overpowering
rajas and *tamas. Rajas* rules when *sattva* and *tamas* are
weak. *Tamas* prevails when the other two qualities lie
dormant and yield to lethargy.

"One should be aware of which *guna* predominates. I   11–13
will describe some of the signs: When *sattva* rises it is
as if the light of the True Self is shining out through
all your gates (senses). Your seeing is sharper, hearing
is more acute, and thinking and actions steadier, more

precise. When *rajas* takes over your personality it is as if impatience, greed, and longing have sprung to the forefront, as if your own restlessness is compelling you to action. *Tamas* has taken charge when your mind feels lazy, bewildered, and uncaring.

14–15   "The particular state of mind uppermost at the time of your death is the deciding factor of your next birth. If your soul departs when *sattva* is predominant, you go to the pure heavens of beings who know the Creator. If you die in a *rajasic* state — full of unfulfilled desires, excitement, fears, and sorrows — you are reborn into the wombs of people similarly driven. If you die in a *tamasic* mentality you depart in an unconscious state, only to be reborn into a situation of equal dullness and ignorance, perhaps even as a subhuman or lower animal.

16–17   "I repeat, Arjuna, always seek to move to the next higher level (from *tamas* to *rajas* to *sattva*), because the consequences of the various actions are clear. *Sattvic* actions result in wisdom, purity, and happiness. *Rajasic* activities always bring greed, anger, and great pain. *Tamasic* behavior leads to ignorance and dull inertia.

"But also know that the anger and pain of driven, *rajasic* people may be heaven sent, because nothing motivates a person to mend his or her ways as much as the misery that always accompanies desire-driven action. Suffering is the training ground where one shapes good character and right conduct (*dharma*). It is *dharma* (living a truth-based life) that lifts one to the serenity of *sattva*.

18   "Those who live in *sattva* rise upwards, whether in this world or the next. Those stuck in *rajas* stay in the

middle, ever caught up in earthly activity. Those mired in *tamas* sink even lower.

"Remember, Arjuna, the *gunas* are nature (*prakriti*), 19–20 and all actions, whether *sattvic, rajasic,* or *tamasic,* take place in nature. All things in nature are just permutations of the three strands, the *guna* forces — even the mind, senses, and objects that attract the senses are permutations of these three.

"The purpose of earthly life, as I have said, is to outgrow the two inferior *gunas* and reach the serenity of *sattva* — and then to ascend beyond even *sattva*. The person who climbs beyond all three *guna* states is in essence transcending nature itself, and is thereby freed of the natural body, and is thus liberated from the awful cycle of birth, decay, death, and rebirth. This person enters the realm of Pure Consciousness and attains the supreme bliss of My Being, Brahman, the Godhead."

How to Transcend the Gunas

Arjuna asks, "What are the hallmarks of those *jnanis* 21 (wise *yogis*) who have transcended the three *gunas*? How do they conduct themselves? And how do they rise beyond these entangling strands?"

"Good question," Krishna says. "Those who tran- 22–23 scend the *gunas* are in essence watchers, beyond the worldly. Although constantly aware of the inevitable cycle of birth, disease, senility, grief, and so forth, they dwell above it all and merely witness it. They feel no attraction or aversion to any of the *gunas* — no desire even for the calm joy of *sattva* or for the excitement of *rajas,* and no repulsion toward the lethargy of *tamas*. They have nothing to gain by adhering to any of these earthly behaviors and nothing to lose by turning from them. While the waves of *guna* forces ebb and flow, these transcended persons remain calm, steady, unaffected, unconcerned, and unmoved. As they do not tie their moods to *guna*-created circumstances, they cease being uplifted or depressed by their own likes or dislikes.

24–25   "Thus balanced in the face of pleasure and pain, these *yogis* are no longer a party to the machinations of the three forces within nature and in the body. They dwell always within Self, *Atma*. Dualities such as pleasure and pain, praise and blame no longer have any meaning. As they are established in this attitude of holy indifference, to them lumps of clay, stone, or gold are all the same. They have progressed beyond time, space, and circumstance, to the place where the mind is tranquil and ego disappears.

26   "The way to traverse the *gunas* is through steadfast practice of the three paths (*yogas*) I have prescribed: One, be thoroughly devoted to the Divine One (*bhakti yoga*); two, faithfully serve Divinity (*karma yoga*); and three, be constantly aware of this same Divinity in all others and in everything you do (*jnana yoga*).

27   "Finally, beloved Arjuna, be always cognizant that I, the Divine One, am the foundation of both the manifested and unmanifested Godhead; I am the imperishable, immutable Brahman above all, who dwells within all as *Atma*. I am eternal truth and everlasting bliss."

CHAPTER 15

DEVOTION TO THE SUPREME SELF
(*Purushottama Yoga*)

*"The one who grasps this great secret
will become enlightened; all duties and missions
in life and the goal of millions of years of evolution
will have been achieved."*

Krishna pauses as though carefully weighing his next   1
words. "Arjuna, let us now briefly delve into certain profound and esoteric truths regarding My most exalted
nature and the highest goal of all, reaching My dwelling
place. I will approach it through an analogy.

"*Prakriti,* the world of matter, can be likened to the mythi-
cal *Ashvatta* tree, a giant, upside-down fig tree with its roots
high in God and its branches stuck in the mud below. Like
the aspen, its leaves are constantly shivering, always in
movement; and like the banyan, it sends its branches
downward toward the earth rather than upward — and
those branches become firmly rooted in the earthly."

Ashvatta, *the Tree of Worldly Life*

2   "The *Ashvatta*, referred to as the tree of worldly life, is comprised of higher branches, closer to God, and lower ones at the worldly level. The tree's buds and quaking leaves are likened to human senses, fed by the saplike powers of nature, the *gunas*. The downward branches, stuck deep, are attachments that bind the individual soul (*jiva*) to earthly existence. To understand the nature of this upside-down tree is to see the inverted way that humans perceive life.

3–4   "Although the origin and totality of this tree of worldly life may be beyond the ken of humanity, know that its branches stuck in the world must be cut by the ax of nonattachment. When you sever these attachments an attitude of sacred dispassion comes, which is the prerequisite for spiritual vision. Then, spiritual intuition supplants your usual seeing, and your whole spectacle of the universe undergoes a dramatic change.

"But cutting the root bonds is not enough. After the ax has done its work, you must seek the supreme goal of life, liberation from the cycle of rebirth.

5   "Nondeluded people who cleave off their ignorance (their unawareness of *Atma*) reach that Supreme Goal. When they are free of pride and have slashed their attachments, when they have dropped their craving for pleasure and aversion to pain, then these clear-seeing ones enter the light of the Supreme Goal.

6   "That light is indeed bright beyond all light! Neither the sun, the moon, nor star, nor flash of lightning, nor fire lit on earth can shine in the self-luminescence of My realm. Once the individual soul achieves this

ultimate enlightenment he or she is forever with Me and is never restored to a separate existence."

The Jiva's Journey

"I will now explain more about the individual soul (*jiva*). The *Atma* (a part of Divinity) enters into a body in the womb before birth; thus it enters the world of matter. It draws around itself the five senses, with the mind as the sixth. The mind and senses, remember, are *prakriti*, a part of nature.

7

"Like a breeze wafting the scent of perfume, the *Atma*, when it migrates from one body to the next, carries with it the mind and the senses. That means it brings along the intellect, the ego (sense of being a separate identity), and the lower mind; transferring thoughts and tendencies from previous lifetimes.

8

"The individual soul (*jivatma*), because it has drawn the senses around itself, experiences the pleasures, desires, and pains of the world.

9

"People who are unaware of the True Self Within (*Atma*), do not recognize this *jiva* in them that is using the senses. As the senses are limited to the mind level, they are incapable of comprehending *Atma*, which is above the mind. *Yogis,* however, possessing the eye of wisdom (intuitive faculty), do see Me, their *Atmic* Self within.

10

"To obtain this 'eye of wisdom' you must do two things: surrender your ego and purify your mind. Only by accomplishing both of these will you behold Me. Those with only halfhearted surrender or only partially purified minds are not granted the capacity to see their *Atmic* Self."

11

God's Immanence in All

12　"Remember, dear friend, that I am subtly inherent in everything, *everything* in the universe! I am the all-illuminating light of the sun, the light in the moon, the brilliance in fire — all light is Mine. I am even the consciousness of light, and indeed, I am the consciousness in the entire cosmos.

13　"A minute drop of My primordial energy (*prana*) entering the earth supports and sustains all beings. I become the life-giving sap that nourishes all plants (including all healing herbs). In fact, it is My energy that gives rise to all forms of matter and energy.

14　"I enter the bodies of living beings as the warmth of life. I am in their digestive systems as heat that turns food into strength. I am the in-going and out-going breath. These powers are aspects of My energy.

15　"I am in all hearts. I reside throughout the cosmos as consciousness. From Me comes knowledge, understanding, and memory. I bring all these powers, and I also take them away.

"Try to contemplate the vastness and mind-boggling impermanence of the entire physical universe, Arjuna, and you just begin to gather an idea of My absolute permanence. By ruminating on the utter immensity of the cosmos you begin to receive hints of the incomprehensible scope of My omnipresence. I am present everywhere in all this vastness.

"I *am* beauty and bliss, Arjuna. It is I of whom all the different scriptures in the world speak. In fact, it is I who authored them.

"There are two orders of beings in this world: mortal (temporal, perishable) beings and immortal (eternal, imperishable) Spirit. All creatures are perishable. The Spirit is imperishable. 16

"But distinct from and above *both* of these — higher than either mortals or Spirit, higher even than the highest deities — I exist as the Supreme *Atma,* the Immutable, Eternal, Imperishable Godhead. It is this utmost-level 'I' who pervades, and yet remains above and beyond all three worlds (earth, the in-between levels, and the heavens). As I transcend both the perishable and the imperishable, I am known in this aspect of Myself as the 'Supreme Absolute Highest Self,' or *Purushottama.* 17–18

"There is only one Reality, Arjuna, one! Those who know and see this Supreme level of Self in Me know and see the Truth. These enlightened souls devote themselves to Me with full hearts. 19

"I have revealed this most profound and esoteric of all truths to you. The one who grasps this great secret will become enlightened; all duties and missions in life and the goal of millions of years of evolution will have been achieved. There is no higher knowledge. That one has done what has to be done." 20

CHAPTER 16

THE TWO DESTINIES: DIVINE OR DEGENERATE
(*Daiva-Asura Sampad Vibhaga Yoga*)

*"... the cardinal virtues and tendencies that reveal
the real nature of human beings:
their Divinity."*

"I can see your continuing interest, old friend, and will   1–3
now describe the distinctive qualities and practices of people with Divine tendencies and degenerate (sometimes
called 'demonic') tendencies. First, the Divine traits:

"Fearlessness, purity (of heart and emotions), steadfast-
ness (in pursuit of *Atma*), charity (alms giving), and control of senses.

"Sacrifice (*yajna,* the spirit of giving), study of scriptures,
purification (austerity, *tapas,* literally to 'melt' and recast),
straightforwardness (integrity, sincerity), and noninjury
(*ahimsa,* doing no mental, physical, or spiritual harm).

"Also on the list of godlike traits are: truthfulness, absence of anger, renunciation (turning away from worldly attachments), equanimity, and not slandering.

"Compassion, not coveting (no desire), gentleness, modesty, not fickle (no fluctuations of mind), and vigor.

"Forgiveness, fortitude (courage, endurance, 'putting up with'), cleanliness (*saucham,* clean mind and body), no hatred, and no pride.

"All those, Arjuna, are the cardinal virtues and tendencies that reveal the real nature of human beings: their Divinity.

4   "On the other hand are the degenerate qualities, behaviors and moods that render a person less than human:

"Pride (ostentation, hypocrisy), pompousness (arrogance), vanity (self-conceit), anger, harshness (coarseness, sternly judgmental), and absence of discrimination (between right and wrong, Truth and not-Truth, Real and not-Real).

5   "The 'Divine' behaviors on the longer list lead to liberation; the degenerate behaviors lead to more time on the wheel of death and rebirth. Do not be concerned, however, Arjuna, as your seeds are good; you have brought Divine qualities into this lifetime.

6   "Look more closely at degenerate behavior — not to dwell on negatives, but to guard against them.

7   "Degenerate beings, because they have no sense of truth or right conduct (*dharma*), do not know what they should or should not do. There is no purity in them.

"If asked why they carry on in such a detestable way   8
they argue that the scriptures are a lie, that God is
dead or never existed, that the universe is a dog-eat-
dog place with no moral foundation. They contend
that what exists in the world is merely the outcome of
lust, or is just an accident.

"Holding this distorted viewpoint in their minds,   9
they become enemies of the world and serve a negative purpose. Without thinking of the consequences
of their actions, they cause destruction and suffering.
If left alone to their self-indulgence they would heed-
lessly destroy the world.

"Stuffed with endless, insatiable desires, they are arro-   10
gant, vain, and prideful. They live in delusion and
chase blindly after evil (those things that lead to suffering).

"Beset with dreads, they assume their fearfulness will   11
cease only upon their death — which is a fallacy, as
the same mind will be reborn into a like situation.
They are blindly certain that gratifying their own lust
is all there is to life.

"They are bound on all sides by scheming, greed, and   12
anger because, being hurtful themselves, they attract
hurtful people to themselves. They amass and hoard
wealth for the sole purpose of indulging senses and
whims. Grabbing for riches governs their every
thought and move.

"They arrogantly proclaim, 'I wanted this or that and   13-15
I got it! Tomorrow I will get more. These riches are
mine, and I will spend my life making more and
more. I have destroyed this and that enemy, and I will
get rid of the rest of them. I am indeed mighty. I am

ruler of my domain. I love having things of the world. I am successful, powerful, and rich. Who can compare to me? I will buy my way, making lavish contributions to the poor and weak, and revel in my own goodness.' That is how far blindness and ignorance has eaten into their soul.

16   "These degenerates, bewildered, trapped in their addiction to sense gratification, are stuck in the spiderweb of delusion. They spiral downward into the filthy, painful hell of their own foul minds.

17   "Stuffed until choking with pride and conceit, drunk with their own wealth, they pay mere lip service to Divinity. They make offerings to the deities only for name and fame, outward show and self-promotion.

18   "Because they have fully given themselves to the dark forces of egoism, insolence, desire, and wrath, these cruel beings loathe Me, who dwells in their own bodies. They deny My presence in themselves and in others.

19   "Time after time, according to their *karma,* I cast these malicious evildoers into the wombs of like-minded parents, subjecting them to the wheel of death and birth.

20   "Life after life they take birth in similar degradation without ever reaching Me or even reaching toward Me. Thus they sink to the worst possible depths.

21   "The three main causes of this depravity are the so-called three gates to hell: desire, greed, and anger. Any one of them is enough to bind you to this darkness, so abandon all three.

"Those who finally pass by these three dark gates and turn Godward do eventually reach Me, the Supreme Goal. In fact, progress can be rapid once the degenerate person turns his or her aggressive energy toward Me and takes the Divine way. 22

"The function of the scriptures is to guide people toward living a perfected life on earth and repeatedly remind them of the goal, which should be nothing short of achieving Divinity Itself. But those who spurn the teachings and guidance of the scriptures and act only on the impulses of their desires will not achieve perfection and Divinity, only misery. 23

"Let the scriptures tell you what you should and should not do, Arjuna. Know what the right choices are and live up to them. It is simpler than you think. When you, or anyone, is firmly on the road to enlightenment there is no conflict at all between what you do and what the scriptures advise." 24

CHAPTER 17

THE PATH OF THREEFOLD FAITH
(*Sraddha Traya Vibhaga Yoga*)

"Faith comes first ... faith that contains determination, zeal, and momentum for spiritual growth."

"But Krishna," Arjuna asks, "some people in all good faith pursue the right path without having elaborate knowledge of the scriptures. What will be their spiritual attainment? Is the nature of their faith *sattva* (purity), *rajas* (activity), or *tamas* (dark)?"

1

Krishna answers: "People are in fact the sum total of the beliefs they hold in their hearts, Arjuna, and there are indeed various kinds of faith. One's faith corresponds to one's nature, and one's nature is equivalent to one's faith. Every individual is born with one of three kinds of faith: *sattvic, rajasic,* or *tamasic,* depending on their temperament.

2–3

4   "Those of *sattvic* temperament revere the gods in heaven. *Rajasic* people worship power and wealth, even though they may not acknowledge those as their gods. *Tamasic* people worship the spirits of the dead — ghosts and hurtful deities (those with negative qualities and those who do harm) — which again are in tune with their own disposition.

5-6   "Some people, due to excessive passions and desires, invent harsh ways to inflict pain on themselves. In their foolishness they hurt their bodies and senses and outrage Me, the *Atma* who lives within them. They may seem to be endowed with 'faith,' but such practices are harmful to their spiritual growth.

7   "There are other behaviors that bear on spiritual attainment. One's eating habits play a part in it, a fact that few recognize. And the way one performs the three main spiritual disciplines — sacrifice (*yajna*, offering up), purification (*tapas*, austerities), and charity (*dana*, alms giving) — also influences one's spiritual development. Each of these three disciplines can also be understood in light of the three *guna* types."

Spiritual Significance of Food

8   "Regarding dietary practices, know that there are subtle elements in food that significantly influence the mind, and therefore shape mental attitudes. This creates a cycle similar to the situation with one's faith: you are what you eat, and you eat based on what you are. And know, Arjuna, that due to the subtle impact of food on one's mind, sooner or later all serious spiritual aspirants have to face up to the issue of what they consume.

"*Sattvic* people, for example, consume pure, mild, nourishing food that strengthens them physically and brings pure thoughts and mental cheerfulness. Their foods are fresh, juicy, soothing, and agreeable to the body's digestive system. Breakfast is light; the daytime meal is as substantial as required but not more; supper is as light as possible so bodily organs can rest through the night. Only *sattva* knows the real taste of food.

"*Rajasic* people are drawn to spicy, hot, bitter, salty, acidic, and burning food. Like the people who eat it, this food produces pain, grief, and disease, and hinders spiritual attainment.   9

"*Tamasic* people eat old, overcooked, stale, tasteless, impure, empty, and dead food with no nutritional value. This food returns these qualities in kind to the eater."   10

Types and Efficacy of Spiritual Sacrifice

"Contemplate the three spiritual practices (sacrifice, austerity, and charity) with regard to the *guna* qualities.   11

"First, consider sacrifice (*yajna*), the 'loving offering' and 'fundamental law of nature' I mentioned earlier.* Sacrifice is *sattvic* when it is offered up for its own sake with no desire in it, no expectation of reward or attachment to the fruits of the offering.

"Sacrifice is *rajasic* when performed for self-glorification, for the sake of show and the benefits it will   12

---

* Sacrifice as a "sacred life," an offering of devotion, etc. See chapter 3, 10–16; chapter 4, 23–33.

bring, or as an attempt to barter a favor from God. Selfish sacrifice is detrimental to spiritual growth.

13   "*Tamasic* persons offer up empty sacrifice devoid of solemnity, without any solemn earnestness, lacking even the proper *mantras* (chants) or rituals — with no faith whatsoever."

Types and Efficacy of Spiritual Purification

14   "Consider purification, *tapas,* which literally means 'to melt,' as in refining ore. The purpose of purification is not pain and penance, but to deliberately refine one's life, to melt it down and recast it into a higher order of purity and spirituality. The goal is very important; it is not self-punishment but refinement — to shift from human existence into Divinity!

"There are three main methods of purification: the refinement of one's thoughts, words, and deeds — also called the purification, respectively, of one's instruments of mind, speech, and body. When you modify these three you automatically change for the better.

"Purifying one's deeds ('bodily austerities') consists of four key practices: veneration of the Gods (which are all facets of the one Divinity); veneration of holy ones, persons who have so dedicated their careers; veneration of *gurus* (spiritual teachers, older people who set good examples); and veneration of the sages, those who already know *Atma* and have transcended body-mind.

15   "Purifying one's words ('speech austerities') also includes four key practices: truth telling; not hurting; not flattering; and devotional chanting (reading aloud).

"I will briefly elaborate each:

"Always tell the truth, Arjuna, and present it in as pleasant a way as possible. If you cannot do that, remain silent. If something absolutely needs to be said you must uphold the truth, but find a way to do it that is gentle and obliging.

"Do not hurt others through harsh words. Words can be more painful than physical violence, and the hurt lasts longer. Words meant to excite negativity are an act of violence; shun such words. Abstinence from harmful speech is very important.

"Scrupulously avoid flattery, even if what you say is pleasant and contains truth. Promoting vanity does not help spiritual growth. The point is to express (even under your breath) only beneficial words that promote movement toward Divinity.

"Finally, devotional chanting, the regular reading aloud of sacred texts, is a purification of speech that can contribute much to spiritual progress.

"Consider now, lastly, the purification of thought ('mind austerity'). This is more important than the other two refinements (words and deeds), because good words and deeds are spontaneous in the mind that is saturated with good thoughts. Maintain a calm and gentle state of mind and you will not be speaking wayward words or doing unwanted deeds. To develop equanimity of mind, allow *only* good thoughts and noble sentiments to arise in you. This may sound impossible to most people, but as we know now, one can indeed cleanse the mind through constant, intense, direct practice.

17 "When you relentlessly practice these acts of purification of thought, word, and deed with firm faith and no expectation of reward, your practices are *sattvic*.

18 "When you practice these acts of purification to gain admiration or respect, your practices are *rajasic*. *Any* selfish motive to receive a return, whether in this world or the next, makes the act *rajasic,* and this extinguishes its value for spiritual attainment.

19 "When you perform these three purification practices without understanding the reasons for doing them, or if they are body centered, or include sorcery or harm to yourself or others — then your too-austere efforts are *tamasic.*"

Types and Efficacy of Charity

20 "Now, Arjuna, consider the three types of charity (*dana,* alms giving). As I already stressed, it is one's duty to give. When you offer charity out of a positive sense of duty with no feeling of obligation in it and no expectation of reward, and furnish it at the right time and place to a deserving person who can make no return, that giving is *sattvic.*

21 "Handing over a gift with strings attached to it makes both giver and receiver uncomfortable. Charity presented with the hint of desire for receiving a return (either here or hereafter) is *rajasic.*

22 "And finally, gifts given at the wrong time and place to unworthy persons (people of questionable character who squander their money or do not help others), or gifts presented disrespectfully or accompanied by an insult — those charities are *tamasic.*"

Om Tat Sat*

"Although these three spiritual activities — sacri- 23
fice, purification, and charity (*yajna, tapas,* and
dana) — are the most elevating actions going on in
the world, they all have a tinge of worldly impurity
in them, even the best *sattvic* practices of them. To
cleanse these practices, invoke the declaration '*Om
Tat Sat*' as you undertake them. This ancient, three-
word phrase echoes far back to the very beginning
of time to when Divinity first projected Itself as
sound. Each word — *Om, Tat,* and *Sat* — represents
the Supreme Consciousness from which everything
else comes.

"Consider them one by one. The syllable *Om* (essen- 24
tially an appellation of the Godhead) is what spiritually knowledgeable people utter whenever they
perform spiritual activities. This lends a sacred and
blessed tone to their acts and begins to dissolve the
tinge of impurity in them.

"Saying *Tat* while performing these activities (literally, 25
'It,' God) reminds one that all actions are God's and
not one's own. This removes the sense of 'I' or 'mine,'
the ego, from the doing.

"Voicing *Sat* (literally, 'That which is,' Existence 26
Itself) invokes an overall attitude of goodness and
serves as a reminder that the action about to be done
is a noble deed conducive to God realization. Uttering
Sat purifies your own activities and reforms the world
as well.

---

* Literally "Om That Is." In essence *Om Tat Sat* means "God alone is the
Reality."

27   "*Sat* has other shades of meaning and other purposes. Any action performed for the sake of the Divine is *Sat*. To engage steadfastly in the spiritual activities (sacrifice, purification, and charity) is also *Sat*.

"Repeating *Om Tat Sat* creates an uplifted attitude toward any activity. The implication is that *Sat* ('That which is') is both the means and the goal, both the Godhead and the way to reach It.

28   "Finally, Arjuna, know that faith comes first. These spiritual activities must be done with *sraddha,* faith that contains determination, zeal, and momentum for spiritual growth. To do these without this firm faith is considered *Asat* ('not That'), which means the act is of no account spiritually and nothing worthwhile will come of it here or in the hereafter."

CHAPTER 18

LIBERATION THROUGH
KNOWING, ACTING, AND LOVING
(*Moksha Sanyasa Yoga*)

"Give Me your whole heart."

Arjuna asks, "Krishna, Divine One, what is the differ- 1
ence between *sanyasa* and *tyaga*? Since both words mean
renunciation, how does the one differ from the other?"

Krishna answers, "The sages say that giving up selfish 2
actions (*sanyasa*) is one kind of renunciation, and abandoning and relinquishing the fruits of actions (*tyaga*) is
another kind of renunciation.

"Some sages assert that one should give up all actions 3
because, being worldly actions, they all have a tinge of
the impure, the not-Real in them. Others declare that
one should continue certain actions, namely the three
highest kinds: sacrifice, purification, and charity.

4   "Listen, Arjuna, while I give you the truth. Both terms, *sanyasa* and *tyaga* mean renunciation. Renunciation is not a negative process, but rather the positive act of giving up. We are surrounded by examples of this in nature: the sun constantly giving up its heat and light to foster life; a ripened fruit abandoning its parent tree; the mother giving birth to the baby she has carried for so long; students leaving school upon graduation; and grandest of all, the individual soul abandoning worldly entanglements to join Me, the Divine.

5   "The 'renunciations' we have already considered, sacrifice, purification, and charity, are the three highest of human activities. You should never give them up. They all are methods of removing impurities for those who understand them — and purity is absolutely necessary to move Godward, which, as I have made clear so often, is the goal.

6   "Also, as I explained, you have to selflessly perform these three high activities with no attachment or desire. It is essential to know this. The cow is sacred because of her selfless gift of her milk, which becomes the strength of life in other beings. *Yogis* and sages contribute to the purity of the world by giving, not by amassing. This, as I said, is the essential law that governs life at the spiritual level.

7   "Indeed, the scriptures proclaim that the sacred acts of sacrifice, purification, and charity are obligatory and should be performed as long as the body lasts. Those who, through ignorance, do not perform them are *tamasic*.

8   "To avoid these sacred duties out of fear or aversion to physical discomfort is *rajasic*. No spiritual benefit will accrue to that person.

"But when one engages in these activities for duty's   9
sake alone, without attachment, with no desire for
any reward, then the action is *sattvic*. Calmness and
purity are born of this attitude.

"*Sattvic* people, not plagued by doubt and aware of   10
the True Self (*Atma*), are steady in their obligations.
They neither shy from the disagreeable nor yearn for
the pleasant. They just do.

"It is impossible, as I said, for a human being to fully   11
be a renunciate (to give up all action) while still in the
body. It simply cannot be done. But the person who
detaches from the *fruits* of actions can be regarded as
a genuine renunciate. True renunciation is relinquishing all desire for personal reward.

"Those still attached, who do things for selfish pur-   12
poses, will reap their rewards in due season — either
here or hereafter. Their accrued *karma* can be either
bad, good, or mixed, depending on their actions.

"Being hurled into darkness to be reborn as a beast
is an example of a reward for evil actions. Being born
as a celestial being in heaven is an example of a
reward for good actions. Taking birth as a human is
an example of a mixed reward. But remember,
Arjuna, those who renounce desire and attachment
reap no consequences whatsoever of their actions,
either in this world or the next."

The Components and Interactions of Action

"Listen while I explain the five factors that spiritual   13-15
philosophy says contribute to every action: first, the
body (there could be no action without it); second, the
doer of the action; third, the various senses; fourth, the

effort (the motion or energy involved in the doing); and fifth, the presiding deity manipulating all these instruments, including the unseen destiny latent in all actions (*prarabdha*). These five factors are involved in all human activity, whether an action of mind, speech, or body (thought, word, or deed), and whether the action is right or wrong (*dharmic* or *adharmic*).

16   "A common misapprehension is that the Self (*Atma*) is the doer of actions. But *Atma* has nothing to do with any of the five factors of action. The *Atma* performs no acts, no work at all, is eternal and pure, wholly unattached to the realm of matter (where all action takes place). The sense of doership belongs to ego, the mistaken sense rooted in the mind that you are an entity separate from *Atma*.

17   "Spiritually evolved persons, established in the *Atma,* whose minds are free from the notion of doership, understand the True Self Within and are therefore not tainted by their actions. To them, worldly activities (such as, in your case, killing or being killed) are modifications taking place in the realm of nature (*prakriti*). Nature, remember, is really the doer of all *karmas*. As they are firmly aware of this, *yogis* rise above the turmoil and bondage of *karma*.

18–19   "Now, Arjuna, I will explain how the forces of nature (*gunas*) interact with action. There are three general elements of action: knowledge, action, and the doer. Examining these three elements from the perspective of each of the three *gunas,* you see that there are three types of knowledge, three types of action, and three types of doers.

20   "The person of *sattvic* knowledge knows the Divinity of the Self, sees Divinity in all beings, knows the

oneness of all creatures in the universe, and sees none of the separateness that others see.

"The person of *rajasic* knowledge perceives separateness everywhere and sees each individual as distinct from all others. He or she believes there are as many separate souls as there are bodies.   21

"The person of *tamasic* knowledge has, in reality, no knowledge at all, only ignorance. This deluded one clings to the belief that an individual is only a body. To him or her the loss of the body means the loss of everything. There is no subtlety of reason in this.   22

"Now consider the three kinds of action. *Sattvic* actions are those acts set forth in the scriptures and performed without attachment. The person who performs a *sattvic* action does it as a sacred duty for duty's sake alone, not for pleasure or personal reward. There is no drudgery in *sattvic* work.   23

"Work (action) is *rajasic* when goaded by desire for the fruits of that action. *Rajasic* work entangles one in self-indulgent pursuits, and requires an inordinate amount of egoistic effort. This type of action hinders spiritual growth and yields sorrow.   24

"Actions are *tamasic* when undertaken blindly without thinking or considering consequences. No thought is given to the cost or merit of doing the action, and the doer has no notion of his or her own capacity to accomplish it.   25

"Consider now the three types of doers. *Sattvic* doers see it all as the work of the Divine, and see themselves as but instruments of Divinity. Thus completely   26 egoless, these doers are free of desire and attachment. They are ardent about the work to be done, and yet unaffected by success or failure.

27 *"Rajasic* doers are driven by desires for personal gain; they are greedy and destructive to the point of cruelty, and joyous or despondent depending on the success or failure of their acts. They are overzealous and even harmful to others who seem to get in the way. Spiritual achievement is not for these doers.

28 *"Tamasic* doers are inattentive, unconcerned, lethargic, and lazy. Indolence and procrastination are their main features, along with deceitfulness, maliciousness, and dishonesty.

29 "Also consider, from the perspectives of the *gunas,* two additional qualities: intellect and firmness of mind. Intellect refers to the faculty of discrimination (*buddhi*); firmness of mind (*dhrti*) refers to the strength of convictions, resolve, fortitude, and courage on the spiritual path. Listen now as I first describe the levels of intellect and then the levels of firmness.

30 "The *sattvic* intellect (*buddhi*) discriminates between Truth and non-Truth, Real and not Real. It knows the difference between action and inaction (*karma* and *akarma*), and knows what helps or hinders spiritual progress. It differentiates between fear and fearlessness, and understands what sets the soul free and what imprisons it. The *sattvic* intellect leads one Godward.

31 "The *rajasic* intellect also discriminates, but wrongly. It has a distorted understanding of right and wrong deeds, rationalizing that the means justify the ends no matter how selfish or hurtful. This type of *buddhi* is

capable of converting truth into falsehood and vice versa. Greed, passion, anger, and fear cloud its vision. It stays mired in base worldly life instead of guiding one upward.

"The *tamasic* intellect, wrapped in ignorance and enveloped in darkness, simply cannot discriminate. Goodness appears bad to this intellect while evil seems good. It understands life in a perverted way. The *tamas*-dominated intellect drags one ever downward.

32

"Now consider the three degrees of firmness of mind (*dhrti*). *Sattvic* firmness is an absolutely unwavering devotion to the Divine, a deeply profound resolve to move toward and merge in God. You carefully cultivate this fixity of purpose through inner discipline and meditation. You turn all life energy (*prana*) and all functions of mind (feelings, thoughts, and senses) Godward, and then firmly fasten them. Like the compass needle that points north regardless of the direction of travel, this focus on the Divine never veers from the ultimate goal of merging in That.

33

"*Rajasic* firmness of mind is similarly resolute but holds fast to the desires for pomp, power, property, and prestige (or even to the attachment to virtuous living). If turned Godward this resolve could lift you toward the Supreme, but directed toward worldly enjoyment it condemns you to repeated lifetimes of turmoil and pain.

34

"*Tamasic* firmness of mind is born of ignorance, lack of purpose, and lack of fortitude, which results in a deadening inertia. In the absence of discrimination or understanding, the only resolve in *tamas* is to eat, drink, and sleep away one's time. The *tamasic* person ignores the rest of life as if it were a dream."

35

The Cessation of Sorrow

36   "We can also understand happiness (*sukha*, joy) in terms of the three *gunas*. The search for happiness gives impetus to life. All beings join this endless hunt but very few find it. The happiness I speak of here comes only after long practice. Sporadic, halfhearted attempts to achieve it do not succeed. Those who achieve everlasting happiness end all sorrow in life! Listen, Arjuna, to the three classifications of happiness.

37   "*Sattvic* happiness is the serenity of mind that meditation brings, the sweet joy that comes with Self-realization. Like all things good, it is hard work in the beginning but sheer joy later — bitter poison at first, sweet nectar in the end. The fountain of lasting bliss flows from *Atma,* the True Self Within. You can find this bliss inside through *abhyasa,* steady practice.

38   "*Rajasic* happiness is just the opposite: nectar at first, poison in the end. It is temporary pleasure obtained from the contact of your senses with objects in the world. Give in to this type of happiness and you invite the pain that always accompanies it. Rely compulsively on your senses for enjoyment and you rob your strength, stamina, and capacity for growth. Your spiritual wisdom fades. Pleasure and its corollary, pain, are what one drinks in the world; real bliss is what one sips within.

39   "*Tamasic* happiness, born of dark delusion, is a non-comprehending, sleeplike existence, bitter at both beginning and end. The only pleasure in this type of 'happiness' is the meager satisfaction of sleep or the perverse enjoyment that comes with idle pursuits and neglect of duty.

"In short, Arjuna, the *gunas,* the forces of nature,   40
characterize all of creation. No creature in this world,
or the middle regions, or even among the gods in
heaven is free from the *gunas.* The *gunas* and *prakriti*
(nature) are identical. Even Brahma the Creator, the
loftiest of the working gods,* is not truly liberated.
Why? Because his action of creating takes place
through the *guna* material of nature, which connects
him to nature. Consequently even Brahma must
someday cease to exist. So, from Brahma on down to
a blade of grass, all living things are connected with
prakriti."

Prescribed Duties in Society

"I have mentioned the importance of doing one's   41
duty, old friend; now I will explain the nature of prescribed duties. The responsibilities of people in the
various segments of society can be divided under four
general headings: Seers, Leaders, Providers, and
Servers. No particular group of people is superior to
any other, but like limbs of the body, each has a
respective role to play. These groupings are consistent
with the conditioning of the *gunas,* whether that conditioning is from earlier lifetimes or this life. It is said
that people are born of their own nature.

"Consider them one by one. Society's *Seers* are the   42
holy ones (in some societies referred to as *Brahmins*).
Seers are expected to establish the character and spiritual underpinnings of society. Their duties are generally of pure, unmixed *sattva* and are therefore
congenial to a person of *sattvic* nature. This is what
is meant by the term 'born of their own nature.'

---

* Again, not to be confused with Brahman, the Absolute Godhead.

Providing spiritual and moral leadership is generally 'natural' to Seers.

"Seers must have spiritual knowledge and wisdom — knowledge of God-realization obtained through devout study — and wisdom beyond knowledge, acquired through direct experience of the *Atma*. Seers must have purity of heart, mind, and body; and allow no perversity or corruption to creep in. They must possess serenity, calmness, forbearance, forgiveness, and patience — and hold to an unwavering faith in the Divinity of all life. The primary purpose of the Seers is to help transform society's exemplary human beings into godly beings.

43   "The primary objective of society's *Leaders* is to help transform ordinary human beings into exemplary human beings. The Leaders (referred to as *Kshatriyas*) are expected to guard the welfare and prosperity of society by serving the people. They are charged with bringing moral stamina and adherence to duty through courage, fearlessness, resourcefulness, and ingenuity in the face of changing conditions. They must be examples of law, justice, and generosity. They must lead by inspiring the populace through good example and yet be ready to enforce their authority.

"Both groups are strong in their own ways. The strength of the Leaders lies in their courage; the strength of the Seers lies in their spiritual glow.

44   "Society's *Providers* and *Servers* are, respectively, the business people (referred to as *Vaishyas*) and the workers (referred to as *Sudras*). The combined responsibilities and expectations of these two groupings is to prepare, supply, and equip society with the goods and services it needs. Providers are charged with the

activities of economics and commerce such as growing food, rearing cows for milk and dairy products, the honest manufacture and exchange of merchandise, and trading. Servers (workers) are the foundation. They provide the strength and sinew of society by working with, for, and in the service of all segments of society.

"Although there are different expectations of the four groups, Arjuna, remember that the practices conducive to spiritual growth — worship, controlling the senses, and so forth — are within the competencies of *all* people in all divisions of society."

Achieving the Godhead

"All humanity is born for ultimately achieving perfection. This is the very purpose of humanity. Through being devoted to one's duties each person will find this perfection. But take heed, Arjuna, the person who abhors his or her duty can never become fulfilled. 45

"Through performing work selflessly with no attachment to the outcome and doing it as an act of devotion to the Divine, you attain fulfillment and spiritual perfection. The notion that work and worship are separate activities is common but incorrect. Live your life and do your work in an attitude of adoration of the Divine. Do each and every act for the sake of the Divine. Love God in everything you do. Convert your earthly existence into worship. The one who does this is truly a *yogi*. 46

"Your very nature dictates that you perform the duties attuned to your disposition. Those duties are your *dharma,* your natural calling. It is far better to do your own *dharma,* even if you do it imperfectly, than to try 47 to master the work of another. Those who perform the duties called for by their obligations, even if those duties seem of little merit, are able to do them with less effort — and this releases consciousness that can be directed Godward.

48   "Just as fire produces smoke, people's actions produce effects that can be negative as well as positive. No activities, regardless of how good, are completely free of blemish. One should not abandon one's duties even though they may seem tainted. True *yogis* discharge their duties faithfully as acts of devotion to the Divine, and thus free themselves from any contamination.

49   "The person whose mind and intellect are no longer attached to anything whatsoever, who has subdued and gone beyond the sense of self (ego) and the desire for enjoyment — that person has, through renunciation, attained the supreme state of liberation from the bondage of *karma*. This loving *yogi* has become an instrument of Divinity."

How One Becomes Perfect

50   "So learn from Me now, friend, as I briefly profile the qualities that make the loving *yogi* one with Me, Brahman, the Godhead. There is no higher achievement in life.

51   "Cultivate a pure intellect. Free your mind and heart of delusion. Be self-restrained. Give up the ego. Subdue your senses through steady will. Abandon the sights, tastes, and noises of the world. Put aside with no regret the likes and dislikes so burdensome in life.

52   "Seek solitude, eat but little, lead a simple, self-reliant life, curbing your thoughts, speech, and actions. Be

detached, impersonal. Engage your mind always in concentration, contemplation, and meditation on the Godhead.

"Cast from yourself all egotism, violence, arrogance,   53
desire, anger, and attachment. Turn your back on luxuries and property. Possess very little, and shed any sense of 'mine.' Be calm, at peace with yourself and all others. Enter into the supreme state of unity with Me — I who am Truth, Consciousness, and Bliss.

"Thus united with Me, tranquil of mind and heart,   54
neither craving nor grieving anything or anyone, accept all people equally and serve Me, Divinity, in every living creature. Love Me most dearly.

"Be very clear about the crucial importance of love. To   55
love is to know Me. The act itself of loving is indeed the experience of really knowing Me, for I *am* Love, Arjuna! To love is to know My innermost nature, the Truth that I am. It is through this sacred and deep knowing that you gain access to Me and become one with My own Self. Loving *is* knowing God! As a deep knower of the Godhead you actually become the Godhead.

"Do not renounce action itself but only the sense of   56
doership. Thus, even while engaging in worldly actions be but an instrument of the Divine. When you surrender there is no weariness in your work. As you are fully concentrated on Me, you will come home to Me in eternity.

"Mentally cast every thought and act onto Me. Know I   57
am your best friend and only refuge. Be solely devoted to Me. Fix your mind and intellect on Me. Once you recognize that your mind, senses, and body — and all activities performed by them — are Divinity, then your

sense of doership, of 'I' and 'mine,' leaves you. When that happens, you have no concern but to do Divinity's work for Its sake only. Your only interest should be to merge in God. It is by loving God that you rise from the human to the Divine.

58-59   "The one with his or her mind thus fixed on Me can, through My grace, overcome all obstacles. I know, Arjuna, that you are a good devotee and a beloved friend, but if you stay caught in your egoism and do not heed My words, you are lost and you will perish. If, in your vanity you think, 'I will not fight,' that misguided resolve will be in vain, because your very nature will drive you to do it.

"You can do no greater harm than fail to follow your inner truth! You have been nurtured in the duties of a warrior-leader. Your aptitudes, temperament, and disposition are such that you must oppose wrongdoing in the world. Facing this righteous fight you cannot simply decide on impulse to practice renunciation and quietism. This ego-driven decision of yours creates a conflict in your personality. Your inner nature will prevail in spite of your ego. Do not yield to this egoism and disgrace yourself.

60   "A man is not different from his nature, Arjuna, and is obliged to act in conformity with it. You yourself have created the tendencies that bind you now. The law of *karma* is more powerful than your ego. Even if in your delusion you think that you do not want to fight, your own nature will force you to. Following one's nature is the only way to work out one's *karma*.

61   "God dwells in the very heart of every creature and whirls them around and around as though mounted on a revolving machine. It is as if dancing puppets

imagine that they are the dancers rather than merely puppets, and because of this illusion they become increasingly entangled in the strings.

"The *yogi,* however, changes this basic attitude and holds the conviction that all actions are in the Divine One's hands. In this way the *yogi* lives life as the willing instrument of Divinity.

"Seek refuge *only* in the Divine, beloved friend. 62 Always remember the illustrious truth that you have neither existence nor individuality independent of God. Attune your whole life to this truth. Take refuge in Me and experience great peace of mind. Those who do not come fully to Me continue to bring agitation and a stressful life upon themselves."

The Highest of Truths

"I have now taught you the secret of secrets. I have 63 revealed the most mysterious of all mysteries. This sacred knowledge is now yours. Its sole purpose is to lead humanity from the darkness of ignorance to enlightenment, from the perishable world of nature to the imperishable world of Spirit, from the non-Real to the Real, from utter sorrow to eternal bliss, and from death to immortality in Me, Brahman. Reflect upon this daringly and fully, Arjuna. Inquire deeply into these teachings and then act as you choose."

Krishna pauses, "Now listen once again to the most 64 profound secret, the highest of all truths. I tell you this for your everlasting benefit because you are so very dear to Me.

"Fix your mind on Me. Give Me your whole heart. 65 Revere Me always and bow before Me only. Make Me your very own. By these acts you shall discover Me and come to Me. I promise you this because we are forever linked through love, this greatest of unifying forces. This Divine love is both the means for reaching Me and the ultimate goal of all human existence; indeed, it is the pinnacle of human spiritual achievement.

66   "Achieving this is the culmination of all one's strivings. Past good actions, which have been helpful in your Godward progress, have now fully served their purpose. Therefore, renounce all *dharmas* and take refuge in Me alone.

"Giving up *dharmas* does not mean you suddenly become nonvirtuous; it indicates you have simply moved beyond it all. Taking refuge in Me means that you give up the idea that you are the doer; then it is as though all your acts are performed by Divinity Itself for Its sake alone, with no concern about whether the acts are *dharmic* or *adharmic*. When you are acting as God for God it is impossible to do something *adharmic*.

"Through this intense devotion and self-surrender your mistakes and sins (actions that steer you away from Divinity) will be absolved and you will merge with Me, the Supreme, forever liberated from the cares and grief of worldly existence.

67   "Our impromptu seminar on the principles governing humanity's spiritual development is now finished, O warrior. You must not tell this sacred truth to anyone who is not devoted, nor to anyone who speaks ill of Me, nor to anyone who does not care to listen. No one should try to impose this holy information on another.

"But those who love Me and teach these profound   68–69
secrets to people who are ready to listen will definitely
come to Me. No one renders a higher service to Me
than this, and no one on Earth is dearer to Me.

"Those who, although not given to teaching others,   70–71
study this sacred dialogue, are also directly revering
Me. And even those who simply listen to these words
with faith and acceptance are liberated from the mis-
fortunes of life and attain the happier worlds.

"You have been attentive, Arjuna, but have you lis-   72
tened carefully and grasped this teaching? What now
of your delusions and ignorance?"

Arjuna responds, "O Krishna, my delusion has gone.   73
Where my life seemed unbearable before, those self-
created problems have dissolved. By Your grace I am
shorn of all doubts. My power and joy have returned
to me. My faith is firm. I am aware of my true Reality and committed to my *dharma*. I will do as You
command."

Sanjaya leaned away from the blind old king and said,   74
"Thus ends the wondrous dialogue between the all-
pervading Spirit, Lord Krishna, and His high-souled
human friend, Arjuna. This dialogue has been so
thrilling my hair stands on end.

"Through mystical benevolence I have been able to   75
report these profound secrets of spiritual unity
directly from the lips of God — spoken directly to
His loving comrade, man.

76 "I take these not only as teachings meant for Arjuna but as lessons for myself, O King. Whenever I recall this holy dialogue, I will rejoice again and again.

77 "I feel especially blessed to have seen the astonishing vision of the Divine's cosmic form. As other people use memories from their past to help recover a sublime state of mind, I will have this Divine vision of God's true form to help me bring back the glory of this experience over and over again.

78 "Wherever Divinity and humanity are found together — with humanity armed and ready to fight wickedness — there also will be found victory in the battle of life, a life expanded to Divinity and crowned with prosperity and success, a life of adherence to *dharma,* in tune with the Cosmic Plan. I am convinced of this."

EPILOGUE

IT IS NEVER THAT EASY

Arjuna looks directly into the eyes of his best friend, God Himself, and, in one of the most famous lines in the *Gita,* pledges to do as God commanded. Can we therefore rest easy assuming that the great warrior-prince lived heroically ever after? Unfortunately no. As we know, the real battle is always inner — and real life is never that easy.

Recall that *The Bhagavad Gita* is a dialogue in the middle of a much longer story. We therefore have information about what happened following this wondrous conversation with Divinity.

Arjuna picked up his mace and bow and arrows and plunged into the heart of the struggle of life. Fierce,

169

unafraid, he showered arrows upon the enemy, sending thousands into the jaws of death — at times fighting so furiously that both armies stopped to watch in awe.

Arjuna gained fame as the war's outstanding hero. Hour after blood-stained hour, the battle raged for eighteen days ebbing and flowing, its outcome truly in doubt until the last moments when only a handful of soldiers remained standing on either side.

But an odd thing happened. At the most critical times in the fighting, at those turns when Arjuna came face to face with venerated relatives and teachers who were now his enemies, he faltered! Despite his direct relationship with God and regardless of his sacred vow, the great warrior softened; his arrows could not fly true. His fierce resolve dissolved; the sacred covenant he forged with his beloved Divinity vaporized into the acrid smoke of war.

Krishna, ever the greatest teacher, feigned outrage at these crucial moments — on one occasion leaping from the chariot in a show of utter disgust. These displays shocked Arjuna back to his duties. Had God Himself not intervened in this way, the battle, and *dharma,* would have been lost.

AFTERWORD

RETURNING AGAIN AND AGAIN

"Philosophy that cannot be understood, scriptures that are not practical — the present world has plenty of these; it is a waste to talk of them."
— Sathya Sai Baba

"Have a scripure to recite, but make your own path."
— K. M. Munshi

In this complicated, shifting world it is one thing to intend to do something and quite another to live up to it. As waves of change roll through, the setting alters and your mood turns, deflecting you to another place. What seemed crystalline in one situation becomes foggy in another. Then you forget, you lose your bearings and your strength seeps away. That is what happened to Arjuna. It happens to all of us.

But when we read the *Gita* again and again, as all scriptures should be read, the words grow in us. We're first interested in the teachings, and then we become preoccupied and engrossed in the high ideals and ideas it conveys. After a while the process of reading it becomes, as promised, an actual experience of the profound truths it brings. Each time we reopen this ancient guidebook this process repeats. Like a beautiful song, the *Gita* seems to thicken and grow richer and lovelier the more we return to it. Its messages gradually, surely seep into our innermost being, eventually penetrating and prompting every thought and act. It's as if we become a part of the *Gita,* and it becomes a part of us.

Thus fully absorbed, we are opened up to the spiritual energy in this wondrous old scripture. We begin unconsciously, almost naturally, to put the teachings into practice. We actually are, for those moments at least, what the *Gita* prompts us to be: quieter, more aware of our highest Self, more active in the world, and yet more selfless, more accepting, more successful, and ultimately even more godly.

"Substitute thoughts of Divinity for worldly worries."

An experience during our recent trip to India illustrates how being immersed in the *Gita* (or any other high and holy message) can surely impact one's life.

After twenty-three hours in the air and twelve airport hours on the ground, having crossed thirteen time zones and the international dateline (where, in an eye blink, twenty-four more hours were seemingly added to the distance already traveled), we finally arrived at the little airport at Puttaparthi. We were tired and a bit disoriented but very happy to be "home." Louise was like a little girl returning from summer camp. It was late August. Our plan, as usual, was to stay here for six months with Swami (Sathya Sai Baba).

We settled into ashram life and I became completely involved in writing this book. Louise, normally a rather non-domestic person, gladly slipped into her writer's wife role, which in her words is to "hold the space and fill it with love." This meant she moved quietly around our small flat, doing chores, feeding me, making sure the "space" stayed conducive to my writing.

She eagerly joined me each evening to go over my day's notes. We were thus fully and completely absorbed in the *Gita* — every minute, hour, and day — day after day, eating, sleeping, dreaming, and breathing the *Gita* — reaching deeply into those old teachings to hone them for Westerners. The days rolled by quietly and predictably.

But this quiet orderliness was abruptly swooshed aside in late September when something happened to Louise. We were having our lunch. Suddenly her words slurred, her eyes unfocused, and her head rolled to one side. The food fell from her mouth, her tongue lolled, each breath became a sort of rattle. I held her, straining to infuse my strength into her small body, wondering what was happening and what to do. Should I call for help? How? There's no 911 here! Who could I call? We live in a fourth floor walk-up; how could I get her down the stairs?

After a few minutes she seemed to be surfacing from the wave of darkness that had swept her away. Maybe, I thought hopefully, this attack was just a passing incident. But as she came to and we began to talk, the wave surged again, submerging her. "Dearest, dearest, beloved Louise," I whispered as I cradled her, "what's happening to you?"

Our neighbor, a cardiologist at the new hospital down the road, immediately put her into intensive care and began the I-Vs and life-support monitors and other processes used for stroke victims. The blankness in her brain continued to ebb and flow for a while and then seemed to move out. She was conscious now but still couldn't think or walk straight, and her left foot wouldn't work, nor her right hand.

I was sitting on a folding metal chair drawn up close to her bed. The modern hospital ward's exceptionally high ceilings seemed to allow extra space for healing. Her eyes were closed. The nurses quietly moving about in their traditional nurse's caps added to the feeling of composure in the large, semi-darkened room.

In my own quiet, I heard Krishna's words from chapter 12, *"Accept the knocks of life as blessings in disguise. . . . Be unaffected by the bad or good things that happen to you."*

One of Louise's lucid moments arose and she opened her eyes. "Hi," she managed weakly. I took her hand. "We have to accept this is a gift, Weez," I said, not really understanding what that meant. "We have to see this as one of those blessings in disguise." "Yes," she said. We were quiet for several minutes and then she slipped beneath another wave.

A "gift?" What does that mean? The word "acceptance" came to me, clearer now. I rolled it over and over in my mind, "acceptance...acceptance...acceptance." It took on more and more strength each time.

Then I became aware that I was feeling better, stronger now, readier to handle this crisis. I was also a bit surprised to find my anxiety had left me. In its place was a quiet, almost subdued feeling. I felt a sort of still happiness in me. Happiness? At a time like this? There was no elation in it, but it registered internally as happiness. Maybe this is what bliss is, I thought.

The Prasad Zone

Suddenly I knew that everything that was happening to her (us) at that point — or ever — was part of the Universe's plan. I knew that no matter how things may appear to turn out, everything would be okay. This wasn't mere wishful thinking. I knew it, and was sure I knew it. It was palpable. I knew it deep in my physical being. And I was absolutely certain of it in both my mind and heart.

I referred to this mood of certainty later as a "*Prasad* Zone." *Prasad* is Sanskrit for "gift" or "grace." I found out later that *prasad* also means "Divine favor" and "to become clear and calm." It all fit with what I was experiencing.

Indeed, I had *become* the serenity that comes with Divinity. All uneasiness had been swept from me. Does that mean I was Divinity at those times? Perhaps. Krishna would say so.

Not once did negative thoughts enter my consciousness. I was distantly aware of the usual what-ifs (What if she doesn't make it? What if she can't live a normal life? What if I can't handle this?), but those self-doubts didn't take shape. Like wolves lurking in the dark beyond my circle of light, they were out there waiting to attack — but as I didn't dwell on these negative thoughts, they never gained sufficient strength to close in on me.

Now, back in this "real world" assailed by the news-at-eleven culture of fear here in the West, it's hard to imagine a mental state so free of negatives. But back there in that zone, I *lived* it. Clearly my task at that point was but to accept and even welcome what had come, and to perform my duty in good spirits, and to not worry about the outcomes.

This aura of harmonious acceptance had completely enveloped me. Nothing worldly bothered me — the tropical heat, electrical outages in the dark early morning when I was hurrying to shave and get to the hospital, missed taxis, skipped meals — none of those everyday annoyances impinged on that calm state.

An even greater gift: Louise was in the exact same place! Her version of the Zone was to be absolutely sure that all was well and not to worry one iota about herself or her body. Although tethered to the machinery of modern medicine — tubes, monitors, injections, CT scans, and such — she spent no energy or attention on her physical health. She watched with detached interest and participated as necessary, but was totally unfazed. No fretting, no fears; she was in constantly good spirits, possessing the openness and easiness of mind necessary for the healing energy in her body to carry out its work.

It was as though the *Gita*'s teachings had come alive, as though Krishna Himself had come up out of the book to take care of us — reminding us in chapter 2 to "be unperturbed by sorrow and adversity." Or it was as if our own swami, Sathya Sai Baba (whom millions believe to be the avatar of this age, the modern incarnation of Krishna) had reached out to touch our hearts and remove our pain and worry. Or perhaps we had actually been transported, as the *Gita* teaches, into Serenity itself, which we now know is no less than Brahman, the Godhead.

Looking back, we see now that it was our total absorption

in the *Gita's* teachings that really counted, not just the *Gita* itself. The *Gita* was the vehicle, the guide, but it is our fusion with it that brought the spiritual power. Our extraordinary strength flowed from actually living the messages and literally being these wondrous teachings for a while.

We remained in that curious zone for several months as Louise pulled through her crisis and began to recover. I learned to be a passable care provider and chief cook and bottle washer. My *pièce de résistance:* great toast and tea.

During that time we lived so close to Divinity that we all but became It. Some people misread my serenity and assumed I was in shock or in denial, or they would comment that I was "taking it well." Everybody was surprised that Louise seemed so well. (The old joke comes to mind: "You look terrific, you must have been sick.") We knew, privately, that it was due to our being so immersed in the *Gita,* but we seldom said anything. It's hard to explain acceptance this high.

Even now, a year later, with Louise almost fully recovered ("miraculously" people tell us), the Zone is still with us. It's not as intense, but surely present. Maybe the *Gita's* teachings, once imbibed, do indeed last forever.

Krishna's final message comes to mind: *"Now listen... to the most profound secret,"* He said, *"listen to the highest of all truths.... Fix your mind on Me [Divinity]. Give Me your whole heart. Revere Me always... [Make Me your very own, and you shall] merge with Me...."*

At the end of this sacred text the ever-honest Sanjaya finishes his narration of this God-to-human dialogue and is clear that he will continue his own immersion in it. He reminds himself (and us) to return often to this Divine Song, this *Bhagavad Gita,* and rejoice again and again.

ACKNOWLEDGMENTS

The Bhagavad Gita is universal knowledge passed down through the ages by countless hands and minds. This particular version of it is my work and my responsibility. In the course of this writing I drew from over thirty insightful explanations of the *Gita* (see the Bibliography). Certain of them were especially helpful.

The Penguin Classics *Bhagavad Gita* by Juan Mascaro was my introduction to the *Gita* in 1975. A few years later I also came to read *Geetha Vahini: The Divine Gospel* (spelling variations are common in India) by Bhagavan Sri Sathya Sai Baba, which to my hungry soul was like eating food, and remains my principal inspiration.

Then, a few years later, the Ramakrishna organization's fine 1,008-page commentary by Swami Chidbhavananda entitled simply *The Bhagavad Gita* came into my possession and sat on my shelf for years, quietly beckoning but only occasionally being opened until it later became a main resource.

Some years after that, when I made the final decision to write this book, providence moved too. In quick succession I was gifted several books: *M. K. Gandhi Interprets the Bhagavadgita* (especially moving because he so openly lived these principles in the public eye); a pure pocket version of the *Gita*, published privately (and anonymously) in New Zealand, called *Bhagavad Gita;* and a small, well-written *Bhagavad-Gita: The Song of God,* translated by Swami Prabhavananda and Christopher Isherwood (introduction by Aldous Huxley).

And finally, appearing at just the right moment were four positive heavyweights: a 736-page commentary *Srimad Bhagavadgita Tattvavivecani* by Jayadayal Goyandka, an eighteen-volume set of commentaries on the *Gita* by Swami Chinmayananda, a three-volume set of clear teachings, *The Bhagavad Gita for Daily Living,* published in the United States by Eknath Easwaran, and a new 685-page commentary on the pocket *Gita* mentioned above entitled *Message of the Lord,* also published anonymously in New Zealand.

There are other wonderful *Gita* books that contributed at just the right times, but the reason I single out this stack is that these are the ones I juggled on my lap and sideboard for over a year, from which my own notes and therefore this book emerged. One grows fond of something that sits on one's lap for so long.

In addition to those books, certain individuals graciously served as advisers and sounding boards during the development of this book. I wish to thank the distinguished members of my impromptu panel both in the United States and India for their many helpful suggestions and editing ideas: Robert Ahern, Steve Hawley, Glenn Hovemann, M. Nanjundaiya, Jagdish Narain, V. K. Narasimhan, V. Pandit, S. Raghavan, K. V. Sundar Rajan, N. S. Venkatesh Varan, Laurie Viera, and G. Venkataraman.

I extend my sincere appreciation to New World Library Publisher Marc Allen, not only for this new version of the book but for his continuing love for the *Gita*; and to Georgia Hughes, editorial director; Kristen Cashman, managing editor; and the other talented pros at New World Library who again helped make this book better.

I also owe my everlasting love and gratitude to my grown offspring: Kathy, Alec, Owen, Shane, and Julie — all of whom continue to be my teachers.

I am, as always, indebted to Louise, my adoring wife who was given to me to teach me love during this lifetime; we have shared the joys of the *Gita* from the day we discovered it together on the mountaintop at Ootacamund in southwestern India. *"Sisyas te 'ham...."*

I am grateful to Sathya Sai Baba, who not only wrote the inspiring *Geetha Vahini* mentioned above, but also inspired the original *Bhagavad Gita* — and to this day lives it with perfection as he relentlessly teaches through example and direct experience these same secrets daily to the thousands of "Arjunas" who journey to his ashram Prasanthi Nilayam ("Abode of the Highest Peace"). Without Him within me not one word would have been written.

BIBLIOGRAPHY

Anonymous. 1997. *Bhagavad Gita.* Auckland: Sai Publications Trust.

Anonymous. 1998. *Message of the Lord: As a Practical Philosophy.* Auckland: Sai Publications Trust.

Arnold, E. 1975. *The Song Celestial: A Poetic Version of the Bhagavad Gita.* Wheaton, Ill.: The Theosophical Publishing House.

Chakraborty, S. K. 1992. *Management by Values.* Delhi: Oxford University Press.

Chakravarty, A. E. 1995. *The Geeta and the Art of Successful Management.* New Delhi: HarperCollins.

Chidbhavananda, Swami. 1986. *The Bhagavad Gita.* Tirupparaitturai (India): Sri Ramakrishna Tapovanam.

Chinmayananda, Swami. 1996. *The Bhagavad Gita.* Bombay: Central Chinmaya Mission Trust.

Cicogna, C. R. 1990. *The Solar Way: A Reading of the Bhagavad Gita.* Varallo Pombia (Italy): Omina Press.

Davidson, D., and J. Thomas. 1994. *Geetha Vahini: An American Translation.* Cherry Valley (Calif.): privately published (with permission).

Davies, J. 1994. *Bhagwad Gita.* New Delhi: Beacon Books.

Dayananda, Swami. 1995. *The Teaching of the Bhagavad Gita.* New Delhi: Vision Books.

Drucker, A. (Ed.). 1994. *Sai Baba Gita: The Way to Self-Realization and Liberation in This Age.* Prasanthinilayam (India): Sai Towers.

Easwaran, E. 1975. *The Bhagavad Gita for Daily Living.* Petaluma (Calif.): Nilgiri Press.

Easwaran, E. 1996. *The Dhammapada.* New Delhi: Penguin.

Gandhi, M. K. 1993. *The Bhagavadgita.* Delhi: Orient Paperbacks.

Gotshalk, R. 1985. *Bhagavad Gita: Translation and Commentary.* Delhi: Motilal Banarsidass.

Goyandka, J. 1996. *Srimad Bhagavadgita Tattvavivecani.* Gorakhpur (India): Gita Press.

Hawley, J. A., 1993. *Reawakening the Spirit in Work: The Power of Dharmic Management.* San Francisco: Berrett-Koehler.

Huxley, A. 1944. *The Perennial Philosophy.* New York: Harper & Row.

Iyer, R. 1985. *The Bhagavad Gita: With the Uttara Gita.* London: Concord Grove Press.

Kasturi, N. 1968. *Sathya Sai Geeta.* Poona: Bhagavan Sri Sathya Sai Seva Samithi.

Krishnananda, Swami. 1991. *The Philosophy of the Bhagavadgita.* Shivanandanagar (India): The Divine Life Society.

Lal, P. 1993. *The Bhagavadgita.* New Delhi: Orient Books.

Mascaro, J. 1962. *The Bhagavad Gita.* London: Penguin Classics.

Mascaro, J. 1965. *The Upanishads.* London: Penguin Classics.

Miller, B. S. 1986. *The Bhagavad-Gita: Krishna's Counsel in Time of War.* New York: Bantam.

Munshi, K. M. 1959. *Krishnavatara.* Bombay: Bharatiya Vidya Bhavan.

Munshi, K. M. 1988. *Bhagavad Gita and Modern Life.* Bombay: Bharatiya Vidya Bhavan.

Prabhavananda, Swami, and C. Isherwood. 1944. *Bhagavad Gita: The Song of God.* Madras: Sri Ramakrishna Math.

Prasad, R. 1996. *The Bhagavad-Gita.* Fremont (Calif.): The American Gita Society.

Rajagopalachari, C. 1993. *Bhagavad Gita.* Bombay: Bharatiya Vidya Bhavan.

Sargeant, W. 1994. *The Bhagavad Gita* (Rev. Ed.). Albany: State University of New York Press.

Sathya Sai Baba. 1966. *Geethavahini (The Divine Gospel).* Prasanthi Nilayam (India): Sri Sathya Sai Books and Publications Trust.

Sathya Sai Baba. 1974. *Bhagavatha Vahini.* Prasanthi Nilayam (India): Sri Sathya Sai Books and Publications Trust.

Sharpe, E. J. 1985. *The Universal Gita.* La Salle (Ill.): Open Court.

Sivananda, Swami. 1983. *The Principal Upanishads.* Shivanandagar (India): The Divine Life Society.

Subramaniam, K. 1987. *Srimad Bhagavatam.* Bombay: Bharatiya Vidya Bhavan.

Subramaniam, K. 1989. *Mahabharata.* Bombay: Bharatiya Vidya Bhavan.

Svensson, C. 1985. *Bhagavad Gita or The Divine Song.* Tustin, Calif.: Sathya Sai Baba Society.

Vireswarananda, Swami. 1997. *Srimad Bhagavad-Gita.* Mylapore, Madras (India): Sri Ramakrishna Math.

Zaehner, R. C. 1973. *The Bhagavad-Gita: With a Commentary Based on the Original Sources.* London: Oxford University Press.

INDEX

Each reference, instead of simply consiting of page numbers, includes the following:

- The first number or number range refers to the page number(s);
- The next two numbers are the chapter number and the paragraph number(s) separated by a colon;
- Each set of numbers (page, chapter, and paragraph) is separated by a comma, while each subentry is separated by a semicolon.

A

abhyasa (constant practice), 62 6:35, 78 8:8, 111 12:9, 158 18:37

Absolute Highest Consciousness, 30–31 3:14–15

Absolute Reality, 70 7:13, 104 11:36–37. *See also* Godhead

Absolute state, 80 8:16

absorption: in *Atma,* 41 4:10; in God/the Divine, 23 2:54, 85 9:13–14, 94 10:19; in Godhead, 45 4:24

action(s), 29 3:9, 151 18:3, 162 18:48, 163 18:56; attachment to *vs.* detachment from, 153–57 18:13–35; components and interactions of, 153–57 18:13–35; *darmic vs. adharmic,* 166 18:66;

guidelines for performing, 28 3:7; and inaction, 20 2:47, 28–29 3:4–8, 43 4:18, 156 18:30; necessity of taking, 28–29 3:4–8, 33 3:30, 57 6:1; nonbinding, 29 3:9; as offering(s), 89 9:33–34; as propelled by the Divine, 34 3:30; refraining from taking, 57 6:1; reluctance to take, 48 4:42; renunciation of, 28 3:4–5, 50 5:6–7; Self-knowledge brings fearless, 48 4:42; three kinds of, 155 18:23–25; union with God through, 19 2:40. *See also* karma

adharma, 154 18:13–15, 166 18:66

adhi, 76 8:4

adhibhuta, 74 7:30, 75–76 8:1–4

ABOUT THE AUTHOR

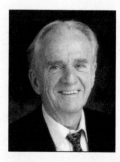

Jack Hawley, Ph.D. lives, studies, and lectures half of each year in an ashram in rural southern India, where the values of the *Gita* are very much alive. When not in India, he brings these ancient yet current ideas to leaders and organizations in the West. His books include the classic *Bhagavad Gita: A Walkthrough for Westerners*; *Essential Wisdom of the Bhagavad Gita*; and *Reawakening the Spirit in Work: the Power of Dharmic Management*.

His website is www.GitaWalkthrough.com.

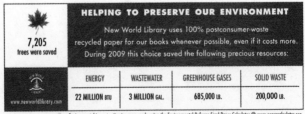